March 1, 2008

Dear Tommy,

This revealing book is about my entire life (and Sandra's), based on many old diaries and journals. My first diary was started when we lived on Carver Creek in 1964 when I was 14-yrs. old. I'm sure my re-collections differ from yours, but I hope you will enjoy this glimpse back into our childhood.

(See pgs 39, 41, 43 & 66)
See also page 266.

Take Care on the Journey,

~Linda

# Dusty Angels and Old Diaries

## Linda Meikle

1663 LIBERTY DRIVE, SUITE 200
BLOOMINGTON, INDIANA 47403
(800) 839-8640
WWW.AUTHORHOUSE.COM

*AuthorHouse™*
*1663 Liberty Drive, Suite 200*
*Bloomington, IN 47403*
*www.authorhouse.com*
*Phone: 1-800-839-8640*

*AuthorHouse™ UK Ltd.*
*500 Avebury Boulevard*
*Central Milton Keynes, MK9 2BE*
*www.authorhouse.co.uk*
*Phone: 08001974150*

*First published by AuthorHouse    5/16/2006*

*ISBN: 1-4259-0723-7 (sc)*

*Library of Congress Control Number: 2006900073*

*Printed in the United States of America*
*Bloomington, Indiana*

*This book is printed on acid-free paper.*

# Table of Contents

When I was three years old, my mother wrote a good-bye note and disappeared without a trace. Her four little children were placed in the custody of the State of New York. Separated from our older brother and sister, my sister and I grew up fleeing from child protective service workers who only saw a glimpse of the conditions in which our grandmother was raising us after she also illegally took us from the orphanage.

This book is about my life based on 45 years of old diaries that re-live the abuse and pain suffered at the hands of an unbridled angry woman; the slow death of a turbulent marriage; the birth and blessings of two wonderful sons; the lifelong search for my mother – and the pivotal moment when I found her almost 40 years later.

This autobiography is not about the ancestry of the Brantley family, the Mascunana family or the Cash family. It is about innocence and power. It is about weakness and strength. It is about those who helped create the paths I took.

I must write this so that my children will know the journey I traveled before they were born. My mother will understand why I can forgive her. My brothers and sisters will know who I am! It is a gift to myself and a legacy to the future!

# *Dedication*

Dedicated to Jim - The True Love of my Life.
Without you, I would not have written this book.
I am and will always be - Your Angelwings!

To my children Billy and Philip,
You are the Joys of my life.
Both of you are following your dreams
And each of you are married to perfect mates!
Katie Yoshihara for Billy and Shelley King for Philip

To my sister Sandra,
You will always have
A safe haven in my heart!
Thank-you to my editor and faithful friend
Marian Mendel

# *She Left One Small Note*

Where is my mother in this world?
She left so long ago,
And all I have is one small note
That's treasured more than gold.
"I've had to go away awhile," she said.
"I hope the days I'm gone are few.
Kiss Sissy and take good care of her.
I will not forget about you!
Who ever reads this note to my babies dear,
Please kiss them both and tell them not to fear."
Where is my mother in this world?
I've wondered since a child.
Did she go away expecting to return?
Or did she go away not knowing where to turn?
Has she thought of me and sister Sandra too?
Has she looked in vain and found the options few?
I love you, mom, though I'm a mother and a wife.
I took good care of Sissy.
But we've missed you all our life.
Where is our mother in this world?
She left so long ago.
And all we have is one small note.
That's treasured more than gold.

~Linda Cash (1986)

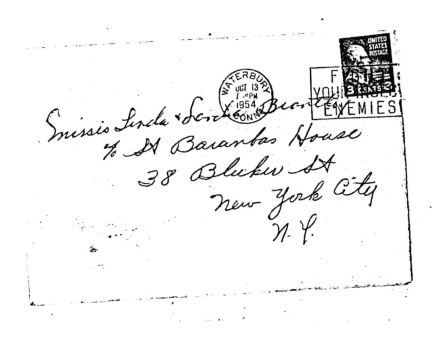

*"This letter lay forgotten in our file at the orphanage in New York City for 36 years."*

# Chapter 1

## *Our Mother's Grief*

She hurried along in the gathering darkness on the cold October evening. Fear clutched at her heart. Her shoulder bent with the weight of her sadness. All the tears in the world would never erase the pain of leaving her four small children in the city that never sleeps.

Would Dorothyann ever gather baby Sandra into her arms and sing soft lullabies? Or would she ever wave 9-year old Thomas off to school again? Would 7-year old Allison come skipping into the kitchen for a cool glass of milk? Would 4-year-old Linda with her dark brown eyes and dark ringlets of hair remember a mother's touch at end of day?

Three months before, on August 12, 1954, Linda and Sandra, her two smallest children, had been placed at Saint Barnabas House, a temporary shelter for women and children in New York City.

Alison and Thomas were placed at the Edwin Gould Services for Children, Lakeside School in New York City since they were older and needed to be in school.

Records do not indicate who put the children into these homes or why. Would they remember a beautiful young dark-haired woman who sang sweet songs to them?

Slipping open the latch of the small rented room, Dorothyann felt the icicles of loneliness reach from the shadows and tighten around her. She unconsciously brushed the soft brown curls from her face wet with tears as she sat at the table and began to write a letter that would be postmarked 7 p.m. October 13, 1954.

She swallowed the acid in her throat, a bitter reminder that she was two months pregnant with her fifth child, and she was only 24-years old. The baby was due in June of 1955. Her hand trembled as she wrote the letter to Linda and Sandra that would lie forgotten in orphanage files for over 30 years.

*"My Dearest Daughters,*

*I guess you think your mother has forgotten you. I have not. Mother had to go away for a while and did not know she would be gone so long. I hope that you are being my good (girls) and that your daddy will write to you too.*

*Linda, are you taking good care of Sandra for me? I hope that by next week I will have a permanent address and will get in touch with Miss Hall as to where I can be reached.*

*Please tell Miss Hall that I have not forgotten my children and will explain when I get in touch with her sometime next week.*

*I also hope that I can see you soon. Be my good girls, and love your sister and please do not forget your mother or daddy.*

*I promise that you will be with daddy or me soon. Be good, my dears. Kiss Sissy for me and I will write you real soon again."*

*Thank-you. Mrs. D. Brantley*

*All my love to my daughters,*

*Mother*

There could be no turning back now. She had to say good-bye not knowing what the future held for her and the small children she was leaving behind. She paused as the sounds from a radio drifted through the thin walls. Perry Como's words kept repeating.

*"And yes, I know how lonely life can be. The shadows follow me, and the night won't set me free...."*

Dorothyann loved to sing. As a young teenager, her patriotic songs had echoed in the minds of many soldiers as they had gone off to war. Her clear soprano voice, sparkling eyes and mystic smile had charmed audiences in churches and theaters in New York City. She lulled many a neighbor's colicky baby to sleep with her lullabies and sweet songs.

But then, at the tender age of 16, the morning sickness started and she felt the life of a child whose father she would never name.

Her nights were filled with helplessness and the days were a blur of nausea, stomach pain from tight girdles and the struggle for a brave front. She didn't tell anyone about the pregnancy. The truth was sudden and shocking as she went into labor on the way to church with her family.

Her mother and stepfather 'adopted' the sickly baby boy born June 27, 1945. They named him Thomas John. Dorothyann felt more and more like a stranger in her own home as her baby boy was assumed by others to be her baby brother. She felt her mother's scorn and her sister's indignation. She couldn't escape her stepfather's covert glances.

As Dorothyann sealed the farewell letter to her children that October evening, she tried to shut out memories of her youth. The son she could not call her own. The scorn of her family, the abuse of her stepfather and, within two years after the birth of Thomas, the pain of hiding a second pregnancy. She swore that her family would not know about this baby until it was born. Somehow she hoped that would make it better.

After almost nine months of anguish and alienation from her family, Dorothyann labored alone for many hours in a strange hospital as the nurses cast knowing glances and told her to shut-up and push harder for the difficult birth.

Allison was born on a cold December day in 1947. A few days later Dorothyann thought her heart would break when she had to leave her tiny daughter behind. Her family refused to acknowledge the birth.

But, Dorothyann refused to abandon her baby girl. Most every afternoon for three months, the nurses would warm the formula and hand the bottle to Dorothyann as she slipped into the nursery to hold and feed baby Allison. Responding to her mother's lullabies and soothing voice, Allison would quickly fall asleep as Dorothyann rocked and whispered sweet promises to the child she had to hide from the world.

After three months, Dorothyann's parents finally agreed to bring the baby girl home, but once again Dorothyann was not allowed to love it as her own.

Allison would grow up wondering who her mother was and why she didn't want her. She would not learn the strange details of her birth-mother until many years later when the siblings were finally reunited in a miraculous sort of way.

As the letter dropped with a light thud into the mailbox, Dorothyann wanted to rush back and retrieve the sad message! Surely there was another way. Maybe Robert would come back to her. Maybe they could patch up their marriage. It wasn't very likely now, she thought. The fights had been bitter, and he had been gone too long now. She kicked a small stone on the path and remembered the moment Robert had walked into her life.

New York City had never seemed so bright! She sang to him and her audiences with a fervor she had never known! At last there was someone who would take care of her.

Dorothyann had married Robert Brantley, a handsome young Navy man who had served his country a few years before during World War 11.

They married the day before her 21ˢᵗ birthday on December 11, 1949 at St. Michaels's Church in New York City.

Linda was born nine months later in September of 1950 and soon Dorothyann held baby Linda her in her arms at St. Michael's Church as she sang, "Sweetest Little Angel", but some noticed a bit of sadness in her voice.

Robert wanted to move back to Tampa, Florida where his family and relatives lived and where he had grown up. She would have to leave Thomas and Allison with her mother in New York City!

In Tampa, Dorothyann and Robert moved in with his brother Bill and his wife, Louise. Dorothyann soon had found an outlet for her singing at the popular Tampa Theater. This time, her songs welcomed the men back from the Korean War.

Baby Sandra was born in June of 1952 but by that time, things were not going well between Dorothyann and Robert. Family members stayed with her all night as she was in labor with Sandra. The doctors said the baby was in trouble with the cord around her neck, but Robert refused to leave work to be at her side for Sandra's difficult birth.

A few months after Sandra's birth, Dorothyann decided to return to New York City to be near her mother who was not well. Robert would stay in Tampa.

Soon after Dorothyann moved back to New York City, her mother, Lillian Silver Cleveland, passed away and Dorothyann's life was plunged into the darkest ebb she had ever known. Helplessness overcame her and she walked away, leaving all her children behind.

After the one letter to Linda and Sandra at the orphanage, no one heard from Dorothyann again. The State of New York would search for her when Sandra and Linda had overstayed their time at the orphanage and people were asking about adoption.

For many years her family would search for her and wonder if she was still alive. The mystery of why she would completely abandon four young children seemed impossible to imagine. Some relatives suspected that she would show up one day and claim the children after they were older and able to take care of themselves. Others insisted she was dead. Robert never saw Dorothyann again.

But, this is only the beginning of my story.

# It May Be You

Somewhere I have a mother whose face I do not know.
There's also a brother and a sister who carry a heavy load.
I'd love to hold them close and say, "Why did you have to go?"
Did Thomas ever make a name?  I wonder if he knows about me?
Does he know he has a little sister named Sandra Lee?
Has Allison worn a wedding gown with little flowers of blue?
So many things about them, I really wish I knew.

I miss my mother Dorothy, whose ghost is all I know.
The mystery of why she left is like the winds that blow!
She wrote me one last letter.  I found it old and brown.
"I must leave my little children.  Life for me is down."

So, if you see my mother, my sister or brother too,
You may not know the hurt they feel because they do not tell
Of what they've had to take in stride, the solitary hell.

It's in your act of kindness – of a smile – a word of cheer
That you have brought me closer to those I hold so dear.
You may not know that you have given a smile I never could.
You may not know that you have helped to make a bad day good.
If you meet the ones I love, traveling down the lonesome road
You have helped to lighten – a harsh relentless load

~ Linda Cash,  (1990)

# Chapter 2

## Something Left Behind

My tiny fists clawed at the gigantic window of the 18-wheeler. I screamed in desperation to flee this awful prison. Trembling with fear and anger, I covered my baby sister with a blanket and tried to hide her from the intense eyes of the burly man at the wheel.

I could see the large buildings of New York City fading in the distance; the tall buildings in the skyline getting smaller and smaller. Sobbing uncontrollably and stuttering with hiccups, I pleaded with the big man to take us back.

"Mo-my 'ill come back. Mommy 'ome back and - and I be gone," I implored.

But the tough, brawny man only mocked my outburst with a deep-throated chuckle and patted me on the head.

Almost a year earlier, our mother had left us at the St. Barnabas Home for children saying she would return when her life got better. I was only three years old, but my screaming rages at any separation from my 18-month old sister had kept us together while the State of New York searched fruitlessly for our parents.

Now this stranger had arrived and said he was taking us to his home. He had installed us in the cab of his semi truck and showed no emotion at my distraught attempts to escape.

She would come back for us, and we would be gone. If only I could get out of this horrible truck. We would go back and wait for our mother!

Soon the sky became dark and I could no longer see the city lights. As I peered through the window smeared with my tears, I knew our mother was in every car that passed by; in every light that blinked in the sky and standing in every window of every house along the way. I felt that somewhere in the darkness she was looking for me. That feeling would never stop haunting me.

It would take almost 40 years to discover the letter our mother had sent to the orphanage addressed to Linda and Sandra Brantley on that chilly October evening in 1954. We could not remember that someone had read the letter to us when we were just babies.

In it, she said she had to go away for a while but she would return. *"Whoever is reading this to my babies, please give them a kiss for me and tell them that their mother has not forgotten them."*

I didn't understand then of course, but our grandmother, Carolyn Mascunana, had arranged for our truck driver uncle to get us from the St. Barnabas Orphanage in New York City and include us in his weekly "load" from New York City to Tampa, Florida.

No one knew what had happened to our mother, Dorothy Brantley, after she had disappeared leaving her four children alone there in New York City.

Our father, Robert Brantley, was separated from our mother and had made no attempt to take us from the orphanage. There was no response from either of our parents. We lost contact with our two older siblings, Thomas and Allison, but we never forgot about them. No one remembered the pink envelope tucked away in the orphanage file!

I didn't want to leave the orphanage. I begged to stay and wait for our mother. It was not until our grandparents gave up hope of either of our parents returning and it looked like I might be adopted out, that they sent for the two of us.

The trip remains nothing but a blur of bright lights that I concluded were our mother's searchlights looking for us. Uncle Harvey laughed at my impassioned pleas to go back. Baby Sandra cried constantly. The trip was imprinted in my mind forever.

When we arrived in Tampa, there was some disagreement over who would keep us. Uncle Harvey and Aunt Tina Kruse were on record with the state of New York as planning to adopt us, but this was the first of many underhanded maneuvers grandma would do with the legal system while she had us.

Our relatives in Tampa had left us in the orphanage year hoping one of our parents would return to claim us. No was eager to take on the responsibility of raising the two little gi ..

Even as a little 4-year old child, I determined to be brave for my sister and watch over her no matter where we went. For a long time after we left the orphanage, I carried a little suitcase packed with some of our clothes every place I went. I wanted to be ready if our mother came back for us!

*I thought that if I was really, really, good, maybe someone would take us back to wait for our mother.*

Because our dad was grandma's son, she knew the family expected her to keep us until one of our parents resurfaced, but the State of New York had rejected her request to take us.

A formal evaluation of grandma had shown her to be unstable, living in an unacceptable environment and having no economics to support us.

But grandma took illegal ownership and spent the next 15 years hiding us in outback places, working us like slaves, beating us to the point of death and trying to control our every thought with strict religious practices.

Grandma seemed to resent Sandra the most and often told Sandra that she was the product of our mother's unfaithfulness to our dad. During fits of rage, she would scream at Sandra and strike her with the closest heavy object within reach.

"You are nothing but a nuisance and aggravation," she would screech and wallop her so hard that my little sister would tumble across the floor and bang her head into the wall.

My pitiful heart-rending pleas for grandma to stop would became groans of agonized demands, but my cries always seemed to increase her fury.

I learned to cover my ears and close my eyes until there was noting left but a pure white cloud in the sky where I would stay until Sandra would brush against me as she hobbled past to hide and grieve alone.

There was no safe place for Sandra to escape grandma's physical and mental abuse. Grandma's fury of hatefulness and resentment toward my sister was constant and savage. We were always on guard for grandma's sudden eruptions of rage and explosions of bitterness and wrath.

The sweetness in the family came from our grandpa, Jorge Mascunana. He was grandma's second husband and actually no blood ties to us, but he was longsuffering and patient when grandma was in a rage. He was kind when she was cruel. He was polite and gracious when she was mean and spiteful! He was small in stature. She was a giant of a woman.

Everyone eventually left us all alone with this authoritarian, heavy-handed woman who was incapable of providing love and compassion to babies who had been ruthlessly torn from everyone they knew and loved.

My sister and I were often frightened by grandma's unbridled temper. We were upset by her frequent moves – often in the middle of the night - to unfamiliar places, and we worried that grandma might one day leave us behind too!

We adjusted to the constant strain in different ways. Sandra was difficult to manage. I was nervous and always anxious to please.

The years that followed were spent being pulled from one place to another. Grandma would sometimes become a screaming maniac who would whip us until blood flowed down our legs as she threatened to send us back to the orphanage.

We lived in rat infested rooms and cold filthy trailers. We stayed in cave-like places near Chattanooga, Tennessee and half built shacks in Missouri.

Sandra and I clung to each other and grew in our love and dependence on each other. Each of us developed the inner strength to survive - each in opposite ways!

Sandra collects antiques. I collect angels. I'm devoted to taking care of others. Sandra takes good care of herself *and* others.

I spent a lifetime of taking care of grandma until she died at almost 100 years old! Even though Sandra has never forgotten the horrible punishments at grandma's hand, she accepted grandma's belated deathbed apology.

After nearly half a lifetime of searching for our lost siblings and our mother, I found them – and more! My book relives the past as recorded in 40 years of personal diaries that were started as a small child while hiding in the cold attic to escape grandma's savage beatings.

Good for
back page

*Grandma and Grandpa Mascunana*
*They adopted us and became*
*our mother and father by adoption.*

# Chapter 3

## *Deadly Hideaway*

"The little girl will have to come with us."
"Never!"
"We have an order to take Linda immediately."
"Get out! You can't take her!"

My uncle, George Mascunana, held me close and dared the Florida Child & Family Protective Service Caseworkers to come any closer. I was six years old and felt safe in my uncle's arms but was puzzled about what was happening and why these ladies were demanding to take me away.

Had I been bad? Why wouldn't anyone tell me what was wrong?

Earlier in the day, grandma had taken me to the doctor who had gently examined large round blue spots on my arms and legs. They didn't hurt and I didn't feel sick, so I was mystified when he said I would have to be admitted to the hospital for tests. I couldn't understand words like "leukemia" or "rare blood disease."

But grandma had disagreed with the doctor and had angrily whisked me out of the room. She had taken me home. Grandma did not believe in medical science, preferring to use religion, faith, anointing and healing by prayer.

The protective service workers were not far behind, knocking on our door within hours. But now grandma continued to refuse medical treatment and the women were forced to leave for reinforcements.

Following the heels of the Protective Service women who declared they would soon return, grandma pushed Sandra and me into the car and headed out of state.

This was the first of more than 30 emergency runs in five states grandma would make before I was 18 years old to hide us from Welfare Workers, our parents and Protective Service Agencies.

Driving all night, grandma soon had me entered for treatment at Wildwood Sanitarium, a Seventh-day Adventist Medical Facility at Wildwood, Georgia. This institution used natural methods for physical and spiritual healing.

Hidden in the natural woods that surround the serene Lookout Mountain and nestled between babbling brooks and small ponds, I soon adjusted to the soothing sounds of croaking frogs, night owls, crickets, songbirds, and chapel bells from the little church in the Wildwood.

The doctors and ministers who came to see me every day were kind, concerned, dedicated, humanitarian workers. The nurses were gentle and pleasant. My treatment consisted of a holistic approach rather than medication and pills. There is no information of what I was treated for, or how soon I responded to the gentle medical care, but I remember the daily prayer meetings and anointing at my bedside. I was given tall glasses of grape juice with a raw egg mixed in so often that I rather learned to enjoy the taste!

Sandra did not fare so well. It was the first time in my life that I was not able to protect my defiant little sister from grandma's intense temper and terrible beatings.

Grandma found living quarters in a small cave across the highway from Wildwood. There was a creek that ran through the back of the subterranean room and railroad tracks ran over the top of the shelter. It was damp, dark, noisy and frightening!

While I slept in a warm bed, enjoyed hot nourishing meals and tender loving care, Sandra's experience with grandma was worse than imaginable. Sandra still recalls the suffocating moments when grandma held her head under the water in the back of the cavern during a fit of rage at something the tiny five-year old had done.

When the blue spots on my arms and legs faded and didn't return, everyone praised God. I kept my little white bathrobe one of the nurses gave to me and said goodbye to a sweetness that would stay close to my heart for many years.

# Chapter 4

## *An Angel to Help Me Sleep*

Grandma relocated to a small Seventh-day Adventist (SDA) settlement near the top of Lookout Mountain and was soon teaching a small classroom of children who lived on the mountaintop.

We were left alone long hours in a roach infested house littered with bugs, spiders and scampering mice! The worst times were at night when the house became alive with night things.

It is there that I learned to pray, "What Time I Am Afraid, I Will Trust in Thee" as the mice scurried across my bed at night and roaches skittered across the floor.

After the soft warm bed and quiet forest sounds at Wildwood, I was not prepared for the bone-chilling cold and awful pests at night. Even the warmth of Sandra cuddled close and my comforting words to reassure her, were not enough to quiet my racing heart.

One night long after Sandra was asleep beside me, a hungry mouse kept nibbling at my ear and several raced across my feet. Prayer did not seem to be working. If I turned on the light, I knew hundreds of big cockroaches would disappear into the cracks along the wall. If I cried out for grandma, she wouldn't answer.

Suddenly I felt a calming peacefulness in the room. My body relaxed, and I slowly turned toward the window. There outlined against the blackness of the night, I saw the bright light of an angel kneeling in prayer. No words were spoken, but a soothing sleepiness overcame me and I was able to sleep untroubled as long as we lived in that house.

Grandma was a teacher for some of the children who lived on the mountain including Tommy Doss, whose father, Desmond T. Doss, was awarded the Congressional Medal of Honor. We made friends with many beautiful people there who dearly loved Sandra and me. They always treated us with kindness when we needed it most. We still remember the Derryberry family and a good woman named Mary who often invited us for delicious home-cooked meals.

I wish I could remember more about the families that lived in Rising Fawn, Georgia when Sandra and I were pre-school age. I suspect most folks thought grandma was a godly woman and a hard worker. Maybe someone will remember two little girls, Linda and Sandra, and know that we survived.

Grandma never stayed in one place long enough for her past or our family to catch up with us. It wasn't long before grandma left the mountain school. As she packed the car, Sandra and I curled up in the back seat, entwined for warmth, comfort and endurance until grandma reached our next destination.

Sometimes grandpa was with us, but most of the time he stayed with his brothers and sisters in Tampa who needed him to work at the family owned Mascunana Print Shop in Ybor City near Tampa.

For a while we lived in project apartments at Waycross, Georgia where I remember playing in the warm rain. Sandra says I had a little boyfriend named Dwight who was later hit and killed by a school bus.

In another southern town, we lived in a house next to the school where grandma was a one-room teacher again. She always taught for the Seventh-day Adventist Church. Early on, we spent many cold December days collecting money for the church's annual Harvest Ingathering. We still remember what we had to say at the door of each house.

"We're collecting money for the poor and needy. Would you please help?"

Later, we saw grandma taking the money from our Ingathering cans heavy with coins and bulging with bills. Instead of letting us present our cans in church with the other little kids, she kept the money and told the pastor that someone stole it from our house.

We also remember grandma steaming open letters from our father and taking out dollar bills before she resealed the letter and marked it, "return to sender."

We knew that grandma was in contact with our dad. She said he was in California. But when I was about seven years old, he came to see us in Waycross, Georgia. He brought a woman named Dee for us to meet. It was the first personal contact we had with either of our parents since we had been taken from New York City. We can't remember details of the surprise visit, but we know that he brought each of us a doll.

Sandra's doll had blue-eyes and red hair. She named her doll Judy. My doll was a bride doll with a long white lacy dress and had eyes that opened and closed. I named her Susan.

Daddy left without taking us with him. Grandma said Dee didn't like Sandra! We heard no more from our dad for almost ten years, and grandma eventually left our beloved dolls behind during one of her many unplanned and hurried moves.

# Chapter 5

## *Butterfly Kisses and Silver Coins*

About the time I was nine years old, grandma ventured back to Florida. She settled at Avon Park and we lived in the old Army barracks at Walker Memorial Hospital. Grandma was in charge of the hydrotherapy department.

We often watched her give hydro treatments to patients and sometimes she turned the strong hot water jets on us or put us into a steaming sauna tent if she thought we were getting sick. Many of the patients grandma treated in the therapy department were wealthy patrons who showered Sandra and me with expensive clothes, toys and gifts.

Our apartment in the barracks was really one large room divided with tall closets. Each closet was about the size of a casket. It was an unusual looking apartment where the walls didn't touch the ceiling and nothing was private, but there was plenty of space for storage!

Sandra remembers Mrs. Bessler as her first and second grade teacher. I remember a near-drowning experience in the lake in front of the hospital. Again, I believe my angel was beside me and supervised my rescue from an unexpected source.

Swimming and playing in the lake was one of the few fun activities grandma sometimes allowed after school. We had begged grandma to let us go swimming with one of our friends whose mother said she would watch us. We didn't know that no one in the group could swim!

Laughing together and splashing each other, we had no idea there was a large sinkhole in the area where we were playing. One moment I was chasing a minnow, the next second my head was entombed in a mass of swirling water!

I frantically flailed my arms and kicked my legs trying to reach the surface. My body screamed in agony for a breath of air, but every time my head broke the surface, I was pulled back under before I could quiet my screams and take a breath. I couldn't get my body to move upward!

Then, I remember just letting go and drifting peacefully down. Surrendering to the massiveness that encased me, I wasn't afraid or struggling anymore. Slowly, slowly, slowly I drifted and felt my body float downward to one side. No pictures of the past. No bright light of the future. But suddenly, with a swoosh I was back. My lungs were free to inhale, and I was gulping deep breaths of fresh air! On shore, I sputtered, gagged and tried to raise my head. I was exhausted and in shock, but alive and glad to see my sister crying there beside me.

My rescue was attributed to a young man who was a patient at the hospital. He was resting outside and heard the commotion at the lake and came running. Diving into the water, heedless of the pain and stitches from recent surgery, he rescued me and another girl who had also stepped into the hole. They said I had come up screaming three times, but she hadn't come up once. Both of us survived.

At Avon Park, we were left alone most afternoons until grandma got home from work. It seemed we could never get by one day without doing something that resulted in a whipping when she got home.

One time a repairman was working on the sewer pipes that ran through our bedroom. We were supposed to be taking a nap until grandma got home, but the man was using a flame of fire to make a shiny liquid (solder) that he was pouring on the pipes. It was irresistible not to stand and watch him mix that hypnotic silver liquid.

Somehow grandma found out that we had not stayed in bed, and the sting of the whipping I received that afternoon lingers today. Over and over the slap of the metal spatula slammed against my legs sending my body into spasms of pain so intense I thought I would go crazy if she struck me one more time.

I tried to control the insanity of my mind as I begged and screamed for her to stop. My head was dizzy and my body helpless and limp but she continued the savage beating until her anger was sated.

The scars from those violent beatings remain deep in our legs and backs today. The memory of the merciless, excruciating and torturous treatment at grandma's hands is difficult for Sandra or me to express without feelings of resentment and anger.

We prefer to reminisce about the occasional weekend when grandpa would insist we come to Tampa. Every Friday, Sandra and I would cross our fingers and toes and do everything we could think of to please grandma. We desperately hoped she would be agreeable with grandpa and drive the 80 miles to visit him and his large houseful of Spanish brothers and sisters.

Sometimes grandpa would come to Avon Park on the bus and spend the weekend with us, but the happiest times were with his Spanish family where the happy chatter was mostly unintelligible, but the actions and body language were clearly accepting!

The big white house at 1209 15th Avenue in Tampa was home to all of grandpa's brothers and sisters who had not married. A little sidewalk ran to the back door where everyone gathered in the huge living room to eat at the long table covered with tempting Spanish and American food three times a day.

Grandpa's relatives would greet us with arms outstretched and squeeze us tight with hugs and kisses. We knew Tia' Soledad would have some tempting sweets in the kitchen or soft Cuban bread spread with delicious butter.

On Saturdays we played on the fast merry-go-rounds and climbed giant monkey bars at Lowery Park. Sometimes we set out for a beachside picnic where we gorged ourselves on hot dogs, chips and pop as we built castles in the wet sand. Or, we visited Uncle Ricardo's ice-cream store near grandpa's house, and spent long moments selecting a favorite ice-cream dessert.

In the evenings after a delicious Spanish-style supper, everyone would gather in the living room to watch funny shows on the black and white television. The men sat in tall rocking chairs and talked of news and business while the women gave Sandra and me undivided attention.

Bedtime at grandpa's house was hugs and kisses time. We would walk around the room and kiss everyone goodnight. Our uncles would press silver coins into our tiny hands as they pecked us on each cheek.

Tia Soledad and Tia Dolores would run foamy, sweet-smelling bath water and wash our backs then wrap us in soft warm towels before we got dressed in dainty nightgowns and were tucked gently into bed with more kisses and hugs.

Sometimes before coming home on Sunday, we would visit Aunt Tina and Uncle Harvey who had nine kids by now. They were a bit wild but always fun and playful.

Christmas time at grandpa's house was a combination of mystery, delicious food and many chattering Spanish relatives who made us laugh.

Especially entertaining was someone we called, "The Funny Man." He liked to tease and play tricks. One Christmas, he poured wine into our grape juice at the dinner table (a Spanish tradition). I don't know which was the most funny, our drinking it or grandma finding out we drank it when she couldn't react in her usual outrage. We hoped she would forget about it before we got back home.

The front living room of grandpa's people's house was used exclusively for the Christmas Season. The tall sparkling Christmas tree would appear magically overnight and after that we would always walk respectfully past the laundry room where we knew all the presents were hidden. Only the "little kids" didn't know that secret!

Christmas morning Santa would appear just as we peeked around the corner to see how many presents we had under the tree. One by one our gifts were placed on our overflowing laps and opened amid squeals of delight. Everyone got everything they had wished for – and more!

Sadly, Grandpa Mascunana and all his brothers and sisters have passed away.

Manuel Mascunana (December 27,1891 – August 1, 1967)
Dolores Mascunana (March 11,1888 – October 1967)
Joaquin Mascunana (1890 – June 1970)
Rafael Mascunana (May 28, 1883 – August 1970)
Ricardo Mascunana (March 13, 1893 – April 1971)

Miguel (July 29, 1899 - August 1977)

Soledad (December 1, 1894 - April 1987)

Jorge Mascunana (Grandpa) (May 8, 1896 - November 1980)

Carolyn Mascunana (Grandma) (August 26, 1904 – March 11, 1997)

Robert Eugene Brantley (My dad) (January 17, 1924 – August 19, 2000).

By the time I finished the 4th grade at Avon Park, grandma was complaining that we were getting too worldly. She said her hydrotherapy patients were spoiling us with expensive gifts of fashionable clothing and expensive toys.

Perhaps our dad was making too much contact and family members were asking too many questions about unexplained bruises, black eyes, contusions and lacerations.

Maybe there was news about our mother's whereabouts. Our cousins told us that the State of New York sent a letter to Aunt Tina and Uncle Harvey regarding our mother. It was assumed they had adopted us as indicated on court paperwork.

Unknown to anyone, grandma was in contact with an old friend, Esther Westbrook. They had gone to school together many years before and shared the same religion. Esther offered grandma a way to escape the heat of family questions and to hide us once again from our parents and the welfare department.

Grandma was about to make a decision that would change our lives forever.

# Chapter 6

## A Woman Screaming in the Woods

"I'll pay you a dime to walk with me to the outhouse."

"You should have gone before it got dark."

"But I have to go real bad and I hate that cold chamber pot."

"I'll go with you if you pay me a quarter and carry the waterbucket next time."

The deal made, Sandra and I held hands and walked carefully on the path that led to the outhouse in the woods. We carried a kerosene-filled lantern that flickered in the darkness. We were careful to watch for slithering snakes, sharp stones or chicken poop that would squish between our toes. We shivered in the chill of the night and from the haunting fear that comes when you are in a strange, unfamiliar place.

How quickly our lives had changed from the comforts of home in sunny Florida where we went swimming most every day, enjoyed the camaraderie of playmates, and were finally enrolled in a formal school.

I had been anticipating 5th grade, joining Pathfinder Club, going on school field trips and having slumber parties with my friends.

Suddenly on a Saturday night, Uncle Harvey had showed up with his 18-wheeler semi, and we were packed into the back of the suffocatingly hot truck. Grandma had decided to leave Avon Park without warning as she had done so many times in our young lives.

This time we begged to say goodbye to our friends and pack some of our personal effects. I especially wanted to contact my chum Susan who had the same birthday as I did and who had shared so many of her fine toys and dolls with me. I was not allowed to call Susan and forever lost contact with her. We had to leave behind everything we owned and everyone we loved - without a word of explanation.

We traveled north over 1,000 miles to a small settlement deep in the Ozark Mountains of Missouri,

Surviving in the Ozark Mountains was not easy. At first, we had no contact with any of our family and friends. We struggled to stay warm and we were often very hungry. The unfinished house we lived in had no electric or water and was surrounded by an impenetrable wild forest and the wild raging waters of Carver Creek.

Memories of a warm bathroom where we could take a bubble bath before bedtime (and where, if one had to pee in the middle of the night, the light in the hall would welcome the trip to the toilet) were fading.

Flashbacks of hot meals and tasty desserts at grandpa's house in Tampa were quickly banished from our minds because of the stomachache they produced.

We missed grandpa and his loving family more than we would admit, but our whimperings were silenced by grandma's swift, brutal reaction.

Sandra would be knocked almost senseless or whipped with a splintery board until she was almost crazed with pain. With the first strike, Sandra would try to stand strong and unafraid, but it was impossible to remain resolute and defiant against grandma's almost demonic beatings on her tiny delicate body.

I would tearfully implore grandma to stop, begging and pleading with every fiber of my being for her to quit hurting my baby sister, but Sandra and I both knew that grandma never let up until she had exhausted herself.

Showing an indomitable spirit, Sandra would hold her moans of suffering and tears of agony until she could hide away out of sight of grandma and me. She would limp away, blood flowing from her tender arms, back and legs, leaving a trail of bright red. She had deep wounds that would be broken open before they had time to heal, and scars that would remain throughout her life.

We figured grandma had moved out here to keep our mother and father from finding us and she couldn't have done a better job of secluding us from society.

Grandpa's family missed our weekend holidays with them and were very concerned for their very special grandchildren.

We missed grandpa's family incredibly! We had become accustomed to the weekend catering by Tia Dolores and Tia Soledad who were so short they had to stand on stools to cook the homemade Spanish beans and yellow rice. We had always looked forward to the times we could walk with grandpa to the little market on the corner to get a three-foot long loaf of soft delicious Cuban bread.

The fresh clean sheets at their house smelled like roses, and our little nightgowns were lovingly washed and pressed by Dolores. We had a closet full of pretty play clothes and lots of frilly dresses to wear to special places with grandpa's family.

Against grandpa's wishes, grandma had taken us to this small community of about five families located about 100 miles south of St. Louis. She had joined her longtime friend, Esther, where they needed a teacher for the few children living far from the type of the civilization we had become accustomed to in Avon Park. We were adjusting to some extreme changes in our life.

Quickly finishing our outhouse tinkle, Sandra and I made a final dash back to the house and we jumped into our bed with a shiver and hoot of relief.

Suddenly, we were silenced by an ear piercing, hair-raising, howling scream in the woods at the edge of our yard. It ended with a long deep-throated bloodthirsty growl.

It sounded like a woman being eaten alive by a man-eating tiger!

The bloodcurdling scream reverberated through the darkness over and over again and seemed almost at our bedroom window!

Sandra and I dashed under the covers and pulled the pillow over our heads. We held each other tight, trembling with fear, too scared to breathe!

I silently prayed my comforting, "What Time I Am Afraid, I Will Trust in Thee" prayer with a vengeance over and over again throughout the long night until the faint rose-colored sunrise gave light to our room and no wild animal crouched in the corner.

Later, the old timers told us we had heard the scream of a female cougar in heat. They are also known as mountain lions. Many have questioned if cougars roam the Ozark Mountains, but we are here to tell you that back in 1964, there was a hot female cougar in our back yard!

# Chapter 7

## *Ribbons of Snow on Our Bed*

Our first house in Missouri became known as David's House because Esther's son, David had started building it before he decided that he didn't want to live there and had moved to Gentry, Arkansas.

We probably would have died had it not been for the friendship and kindness of the few people who lived within walking distance along Carver Creek near Annapolis, Missouri.

The pets, it seemed had better living quarters than we did. The cat and dog shared an old weatherworn doghouse while Sandra and I wore threadbare coats to bed and huddled together to keep warm during those bitterly cold winter nights when the wind chill was 40 below. We knew that if it snowed during the night, we would wake to find tiny threads of snow that had drifted through the cracks in the walls and rested on our bed.

Grandma, stout and tough, would pile her bed high with old clothes and rags and snore the rafters loose! Grandpa refused to endure the cold winters and remained with his family in Tampa.

Sandra's little kitten, still wet from birth when we piled into Uncle Harvey's big truck, sucked on her baby bottle of Carnation Pet canned milk and snuggled close under the covers.

Sambo was born the night before we left Tampa and our cousins gave him to Sandra as we pulled away. (Sambo later surprised us with three kittens! We had always thought she was a boy kitty!)

When young girls our age were screaming over the Beatles, we were chopping firewood and emptying chamber pots. When, "Lassie Come Home" was a family show, we had no radio or TV.

The Ozark Missouri Mountains may be a perfect vacation spot to weary city folk with its many lakes, breathtaking waterfalls, deep caverns and wandering mountain trails, but we were not on vacation!

Sandra and I knew the mountain's brutal secrets. Deadly rattlesnakes lay on the narrow footpath to the natural spring hidden deep in the woods where we scooped buckets of drinking water.

We might bicker over whose turn it was to carry the water bucket from the insect-filled spring, but we didn't ague over who would go because neither of us would tread the slippery path alone! It seemed we could never get the bucket full enough not to splash on our legs blue with cold, or full enough to please grandma!

Poisonous water moccasins lay sunning on the hanging branches by the creek and dropped down beside us as we bathed there on warm summer days. Leeches stuck to our legs or slid into tiny body openings if we lingered too long. Sharp rocks in the creek bed cut into our tender feet.

In the summer, our ankles were swollen and red from constant fleabites, and our little bodies were covered with itchy red welts from hundreds, perhaps thousands, of chiggers. Mice ate any treats we tried to hide from grandma, and each morning we would scramble to help each other untangle cockroaches from our hair!

Sometimes it's hard to imagine the primitive conditions we tolerated in Missouri, especially the first couple years when we lived in David's house during our pre-teen years.

Our house was open to winter's blast and summer rains. Our toilet was a neighbors' outhouse a half-mile down the path surrounded by spiders, snakes and scorpions, or simply a step into the woods.

The square box of a house was divided down the middle with a thin wall of sheetrock. Bare rafters rested between the roof and us. We had a small sink in the kitchen area, but no water. We had no electronics of any kind because there was no electricity. We cooked on a pot-bellied stove that got so hot it almost set the house on fire! Or, if the fire went out in the wintertime, we woke to find everything cold and frozen.

Instead of a warm bedtime bath, we pulled out the chamber pot. In place of warm pajamas, we put on extra sweaters and even our coats on the coldest nights. When one of us turned over, the other turned too so we would stay a bit warmer on both sides!

Breakfast was usually one pan of something cooked on top of the heating stove. Grandma received commodities, so she had a good supply of cornmeal, flour and powdered milk. She often made a pot of cornmeal mush for the dogs and us. Sometimes we had powdered eggs with the bland mush but most of the time they had run out of butter, powdered milk and eggs by the time grandma picked up our commodities.

That first year we adjusted to many things we could not change. The bitter subzero weather, the lung wrenching coughs and raging fevers, the same tasteless food every day, and the almost unbearably lonely isolation.

We felt desolate and forsaken in this remote and distant land. We were incredibly homesick and worried that no one would ever be able to find us out here in this remote and secluded place.

We were often sick and without medical intervention except grandma's old-fashion remedies. Grandma's cure for a bad cough was a teaspoon of kerosene on a spoonful of sugar. Earaches were treated with warm onion juice poured down the ear.

A pain in my side called for an overnight lemon juice poultice. Sore throats got wrapped with wool and plastic for a day. Deep cuts were sewed together with needle and thread! Skin infections were treated with a potato poultice to draw out the poison.

Unlike the mountain people who had always lived in these backwoods, grandma knew about antibiotics, emergency rooms, doctors and modern medicine, but she chose to remove herself to a place where the people thought she was god-like and where she had supreme control over our lives.

For that reason, we had the unconditional acceptance and respect of the small community that lived along Carver Creek. After the winter snows had melted and the sun had dried the land, we looked out and saw a narrow gravel road running beside our house

# Chapter 8

## Walkabout Carver Creek

Come, take a Walkabout with me on the dusty gravel road that follows the meandering creek and connected the Carver Creek families of the early 60's. Let's go back in time and meet the friendly, hardworking mountain folk who became our lifelong friends and helped shape the rest of our lives.

Or, if you ever want to add this neck of the Missouri woods to your vacation plans, here's how to find that little five-mile section of road in the horseshoe of Carver Creek where we walked barefoot in the summer and almost froze in the winter.

These are the directions from the St. Louis Airport: From St. Louis, take I-70 east for about 12 miles. Then take I-55 south and travel 35 miles to US-67 south for about 50 miles. At the Fredericktown/Arcadia exit, turn right onto MO-72 and drive about 18 miles to Ironton, Missouri.

From Ironton – Arcadia, Missouri, take Hwys. 21 and 49 south to near Glover where they junction. Hwy 21 turns right or west to Lesterville while Hwy 49 continues south to Annapolis.

At this junction, follow Hwy. 21 west (right) and you will go over a hill. As you come down the hill and the road levels off, slow down and turn left onto a gravel road just before you would cross a little bridge over Carver Creek.

We used to call this Glover Hill and Carver Creek Road. It is about three miles down this gravel road that you will cross the creek on a cement slab. This five-mile stretch between the two slabs is the place we lived called, "Carver Creek."

Pull your car over to the side of the narrow road. We are going to walk from here on today.

Let's stop and look at the creek. If the water is running over the slab, the creek may be rising and could quickly become too dangerous to cross. Walk over to the edge of the cement slab. Sit down and take off your shoes. Little brown minnows will tickle your toes as you dip them into the shockingly cold water. Tiny gnats will sting your arms and legs, and the humidity will make it difficult to breathe.

Follow the creek waters with your eyes and you can spot large turtles sunning on the warm flat rocks. Overhead you may glimpse a shiny snake sunning itself on a branch sticking out over the water.

During the summer, a heavy downpour can cause the creek to become a roaring mass and lethal weapon to anyone trying to cross. The rocks disappear, the water rushes over the banks and riptides swirl across the pastures.

Those who live on the other side of the creek know if you are going to have a baby and the creek is up, let it be born at home. If you go to the store and get caught on the far side of the creek, go back and spend the night in town. If the cows have wandered across the creek, let them stay there. If visitors are expected, pray that they have the good sense to back off and come back another day!

If you've traveled a thousand miles to visit the old place and when you get there the creek is up, turn around and go back.

Today is sweltering hot and the creek is a babbling brook. Gnats and minnows are out in force. I hope you are dressed with long sleeves and pants to cover any exposed skin from stinging gnats, chiggers and ticks. No matter how you're dressed, you will soon be drenched with sweat and your hair will be matted to your head from the heat and humidity.

Chiggers and seed ticks are loaded in the weeds and we will be covered from head to toe with the almost invisible creatures if we aren't careful.

I've been checking the Ironton and Annapolis weather forecast on the Internet for several days before setting out on our Walkabout trip back to the creek, so we feel fairly safe to make this crossing.

When you cross the creek, there's a slight turn to the left. Immediately on the left hand side of the road is a beautiful green meadow and picturesque farmhouse. We don't know who lives there now. Probably a weekend hideaway for a rich St. Louis couple.

Moving on down the gravel roadway, we peer through the brush and small trees to our right and discover a weatherworn house almost invisible in the woods. Never painted and leaning slightly to one side on a small hill, the back room that used to be the miniscule kitchen is falling down into the ravine. The slight incline of a driveway has been worn down with the passage of 30 years, leaving tops of large rocks exposed.

This was the home of a middle-aged couple named Vernon and Juanita Estey. If you examine the ground closely, you will find many strange-looking plastic objects sticking up through the dirt. These were sheets of rubber mats from a shoe factory many years ago. Vernon brought home hundreds of these mats that had been used to make heels for shoes. Each large sheet had rows and rows of heels punched out. He used them to line the driveway to try to keep down the erosion. It looks like they did a pretty good job lasting all these years!

His wife, Juanita, would often burst out with strange words or dash across the room after invisible objects. She was diagnosed by the state as legally insane and we were told the doctors had preformed a frontal lobe lobectomy, popular back in those days.

The Esteys were the only family on the creek to have a TV and we would beg grandma to let us walk to their home for special events on TV. Sometimes she said yes and we would skip and run down the road to their house so our permitted 90 minutes wouldn't be taken up walking the three miles from our house to theirs.

Vernon would select one of us, and sometimes he insisted that both of us, sit on his lap while we watched his TV. We tolerated his lap and his wife's strange behavior for a few moments of TV shows like, "Lassie Come Home" and "The Ed Sullivan Show."

The Estey's had electricity but no running water. Juanita kept a large bucket of water in the kitchen but scolded us if we asked for a drink because every precious drop was hauled from a hand-held pump several miles down the road.

The house was heated in the winter with a big-bellied stove in the living room, as were most other homes along the creek.

As children, Sandra and I suspected that Vernon had hidden money on his property. He didn't believe in banks and didn't buy much from stores. Once he spent several weeks digging a mysterious large hole way back in the woods. We sat at the top of this man-made cistern and watched as day after day as he tossed shovels of dirt up over our heads.

Juanita kept a few chickens in a little box-like hen house by the path that led to the outhouse. She nurtured colorful wildflowers along the path and kept pots of blooming flowers all around the drab little home already stained by seasons of time.

When Sandra and I returned to Carver Creek half a lifetime later, we carried large flashlights and crept inside the shell of a house looking for any reminders of Vernon and Juanita. Wild critters scampered out of the flashlight beam and I fell through the floor. Sweat burned our eyes and the dust made us sneeze. I was sure we would find wads of money in the attic, but the ceiling had all fallen down and nothing but cobwebs and asbestos reflected in the light.

Strangely, a few crumbling items still hung on the crackled walls and remnants of furniture were still in place as if the people living there had just walked away.

Next down the dusty road on the right about a half-mile or so, was the Jimmy and Mary Jordan family. They had an epileptic daughter, Lilly, who became our best friend.

This family of three lived in a little white house. It was clean and neat inside and out. Their tiny front yard was uncluttered and handy for cutting wood, washing clothes or cleaning chickens for supper. Lanterns were hanging in every room, ready for the evening lights because this home had no electricity or running water.

The doorway of the tiny house was not over five feet high. It was small even to Sandra and me at that time. The living room was just large enough to fit a miniature couch and two small chairs for the family. Jimmy's fiddle leaned against the wall in the corner. Mary had covered the walls of her house with pretty bits of colorful pictures from the Sears catalog.

She was short and stout, and smiled a lot when we were there. I believe she was the only one in the family who could read and write. She wrote the weekly Carver Creek news for the newspaper in Ironton.

They had a little wood stove in the middle of the tiny, tiny living room and a big woodburning cooking stove in the kitchen. Mary was a great country cook and could prepare delicious meals. We lived for the times after church when she would invite us over for Sabbath dinner! I can still almost smell Mary's hot scalloped potatoes and taste her sweet juicy apple pie.

Behind the house and down a grassy knoll, was a long green meadow that ran along the creek. In the evenings we would watch deer, wolves, and foxes cautiously getting an evening drink from the creek. There was talk of wild bears and hyena but we didn't see them.

Lilly was about 30 years old but happy as a little child. Her teeth were crooked and her gums were grossly swollen from the medicine she had to take for seizures. She wore long dresses almost to her ankles and usually had an apron on over her dress because she was always busy helping her mother.

Mary and Jimmy raised chickens and always had plenty of eggs! I think the hen house was bigger than their home! Sandra and I used to think that Lilly's laugh sounded like the cackle of a hen when it lays an egg. I'm sure not many people today have heard a cackling hen, but you should have seen us run when one of the chickens would start kaa-kaa, ka-ka-ka- kaaa! We knew we would find a big brown egg in the nest!

Early every Sunday morning you could find Lilly and her mother scrubbing clothes in the front yard on a scrub board in a big metal tub of hot, steamy foamy water.

Soon the clotheslines would be full of Jimmy's overalls, long homemade dresses, pretty aprons, long johns, and bed linens. A long forked stick would hold the line off the ground.

Sandra and I were jealous of Lilly's solid forked clothesline pole because it never fell down like ours did. We endured many whippings at the end of a long difficult washday because our clothesline pole fell down or the dogs pulled the clothes off the line or the goat would nibble at something hanging just within reach!

Jimmy played the fiddle like an Ozark Mountain Master! His bow flying back and forth and his foot keeping time with the music always mesmerized us. Sometimes when grandpa would visit for a few weeks, he would play the violin while Jimmy play the fiddle. Later in this book I'll give you a web site where you can go to hear some of the same banjo music we heard so long ago.

Jimmy played foot tapping fiddle songs like, "Piggy in the Pen", "Cripple Creek", "Fare Thee Well", and "My Blue-eyed Girl".

When Lilly wasn't busy helping her mother scrubbing clothes, canning food or cleaning the house, she would walk down the road to our house. We knew she was on her way because we could hear her "hen-cackling" laughter in the distance as she walked and skipped toward our place.

Lilly's infectious laugh was sweet music to our ears and we would run to greet her when she rounded the bend. We knew she would take us for long walks in the woods and show us many edible plants and our favorite (non hallucinogenic) mushrooms. We would come home with tasty greens for salads and mushrooms to be sprinkled with seasoned flour and fried to a golden brown.

But Lilly was prone to frequent massive seizures. Many times our happy outing would end with her having a seizure in the woods or on the road. We learned to sit and wait until she woke up, then we would help her back home knowing that she wouldn't be out and about for a day or two.

Following the creek past the Jimmy Jordan's house and kicking up a little trail of dust as we walk along the road, we see a turn in the road and the creek only a few feet from the edge of the road. There used to be a small wooden two-bedroom shack sitting right by the edge of the creek. This was the Westbrook house where our friend Cindy lived with her mom and dad, Esther and Lloyd.

We never knew why he built the house so close to the creek, but perhaps Mr. Westbrook enjoyed hearing the gurgle of the water as it chased around the tree roots and lapped around the doorsteps after a good rain. Later the roaring creek would wash the house away, but not while we lived there.

I'm suddenly flooded with memories of sitting on tree branches out over the water as Sandra, Cindy and I ate raw peanuts from Mr. Westbrook's garden. The same trees have now grown to be thick limbs and have spread out over the entire creek from edge to edge.

Mr. Westbrook and grandma each planted huge gardens every year. We helped plow the land, plant seeds and pull stickery weeds that made our hands itch all the time. We picked vegetables from early spring until late fall and spent many hours canning the vegetables for winter.

Our hands would be bleeding and our feet covered with cuts and scrapes by the time the autumn winds blew coolness into the valleys and over the ridges.

Grandma made us work many hours in her garden, and we often helped out in the Westbrook garden. It seemed so much more fun when we got to ride on Mr. Westbrook's horse drawn wagon or play in the creek with Cindy after a hard day working in the gardens.

One day, the farm wagon overturned and I was thrown out. The rail post landed in the middle of my back. Suffocating, I couldn't move or breathe until Mr. Westbrook lifted the wagon off of me, and then I couldn't stop screaming. Grandma slapped me into silence and would not hear of seeking medical attention for my back.

A few years later, Mr. Westbrook died when he backed his tractor into the creek and the tractor overturned onto him, slowly crushing him to death while his wife knelt helplessly beside him.

Now follow me again and lift your pant legs as we wade across the creek at the point where the Westbrook house stood. We might find a faint trail that leads through the woods and undergrowth to where old Mary Sutton lived.

The story was told that Mary Sutton's place was at one time a hiding spot for the famed Jessie James. Mary supposedly played with Jessie James as a child.

Mary's house had been a sturdy well-built home filled with artifacts from St. Louis at one time. She had grown up in that house and enjoyed a rich lifestyle far from the city. But when we lived there as children, she was withered and old. The outside of her house was stained by summer rains and many winters' blasts.

However, a few remnants of the golden days remained inside when we lived there. One item I remember was a very old pump organ. Mary allowed me to pump the pedals and play a hymn or two whenever we ventured across the creek to her house.

I'm glad you are taking this walk with me. Step carefully because the path has high weeds and each leaf is full of little chiggers that bite and dig into your skin with a vengeance. These eight-legged little creatures are too small to be seen with the naked eye and must be washed off with a warm bath of soapy water or they will create a large red welt that will itch for weeks!

We often applied turpentine or kerosene to the itchy irritated areas of our bodies, but it was useless because our baths were usually very cold and often without soap!

Tonight we'll have to check each other for ticks too. Especially on your back and in your hair because if you don't find them before they settle in, you'll probably have to pick off a few from under your arms and around your waistline tomorrow.

After leaving Mary's house, we almost miss David's House. The old place has rotted and fallen to the ground. We see only a few metal sheets from the roof and some rotten boards scattered about from what used to be our first winter shelter in Missouri.

The creek has changed its course here because the area where the path once led to the spring is covered with dark green water and sludge from the creek.

We quickly move on to the spot where the Blevins family lived.

You always knew when someone was walking past the Blevens house because his dogs would set up a loud barking clatter. Mr. And Mrs. Blevins had over 20 children, but when we lived there, only four were still at home.

The three boys were shifty-eyed and slinky-looking to me. Sandra thought Amos was cute with his small stature and dimples. Cindy had a crush on David who was short and growing fuzz on his chin. (She later married David.)

Elijah was tall and quiet. Mr. Blevins seemed scary because he always talked fast and loud and had no teeth. Mrs. Blevins, meek and shy, usually hid in the bedroom if anyone came by. Bernice was the only girl at home and she was tall, gaunt, and unkempt. Like her mother, she didn't say much, but she giggled a lot.

In my mind now, I see a playpen full of dirty clothes in the living room and a sagging couch with puffs of stuffing bulging out. Through the doorway, I see bare mattresses on stained brass frames.

There are no sheets or pillows. Only thin filthy blankets strewn about. Nothing is painted or decorated. There are no pictures on the walls.

Through the doorway to the kitchen is a hot wood burning stove and a large bucket of lard sitting in the windowsill. The few dishes scattered around are dirty but intended to be used for the next meal. Several skinny dogs are growling but not moving after Mr. Blevins has given them a swift kick across the room. It was always a strange experience going to their house.

Mr. Blevins was a Pentecostal preacher who spoke in tongues and ordered the devil to leave the bodies of his parishioners. We could hear his yelling and floor stomping church services continuing long into the hot summer nights.

Behind the Blevins house there was a homemade swinging bridge that hung precariously over the creek. Back then, we could sometimes sneak away from grandma as we carefully crossed that bridge and prowled the woods with Cindy and the Blevins boys.

Today, the cumbersome bridge is gone but we notice an uneven footpath leading down the hill to a place where someone has poured enough cement in the creek to make wading across possible. Shall we check it out?

A breathtaking sight welcomes the traveler who crosses the creek here. It is an unexpected paradise of beauty! Our little bucket-sized spring has grown into a dark blue mirror pond surrounded with purple, pink and yellow wild flowers. A perfect little grassy meadow surrounds the quiet pond.

Only those who can relive the faded memory of a slippery path and sloppy buckets of water splashing on bare legs, can appreciate the magnificent splendor now!

Taking a few pictures to savor the awesome moment, we continue our walkabout of Carver Creek from one end to the other.

We pass old cow pastures now fields of yellow. Beyond the grasslands are the uninterrupted green mountain forests filled with Missouri oak and hickory trees. The woodlands are sprinkled with bright evergreens. We can almost catch the cool mountain scent in the slight breeze.

A noise up ahead stops us for a moment. Is that wild animal waiting for us? But no, it's only a billygoat standing on a large rock in front of a fairly modern home. He makes no motion toward us as his mouth works back and forth in a chewing motion.

Tommy Wake and his family lived here long ago but Tommy was not Seventh-day Adventist (SDA) and because he went to the public school in Annapolis, grandma absolutely didn't want us associating with Tommy!

But heedless of grandma's dreadful warnings, he and Sandy were good friends and we usually found an excuse to stop at his house once in awhile on our way to the Westbrook, Blevens' or Estey's house.

Tommy's dad had a little farm and some milk cows. Their house seemed huge to us with its large front porch painted white and pretty curtains in the windows. The Wake family enjoyed the benefits of electricity, water and indoor plumbing!

We liked Tommy's mom a lot because she was nice to us and always offered fresh cookies and milk. One day she left and we didn't ever see her again. We heard she didn't like living so far from civilization. After that, it was only Tommy and his dad and no more soft chewy cookies.

A mysterious mound still rises from the middle of the field in front of the old Wake house. We were always curious about this strange-looking knoll in the center of an otherwise flat piece of land. Some said it was an old Indian burial ground.

We nod to Mr. Billygoat still eyeing us suspiciously. It's hot and he stomps his foot at our intrusion, but it looks like he will not move against us today.

Continuing on our Walkabout, the road goes up a steep hill and around a large sweeping curve. Perfect for sledding in the wintertime! At the bottom of the hill on the left was a big old red schoolhouse surrounded by shady trees and small brush.

In front of the schoolhouse was a community well with a hand held pump. You had to prime the well (pour water into the hole) and pump up and down to get a gush of sparkling cold water, but it was the best tasting – and sometimes only – drinking water around when the springs dried up.

Later grandma would teach school in the old school building. We played kickball at recess in the open area in front of the building and memorized Bible verses for every class! On Saturday nights

Jimmy would bring his fiddle to life and the boys would buy our apple pies.

Today we can't find the old water pump and the unstable building is surrounded with chigger-laden bushes and rusty old farm equipment, so we move on.

As we walk past a small building of gray sun-bleached wood, I point out that this was Albert's barn where I learned how to milk cows without being kicked or peed on. The walls lean toward the east like they might collapse with the next puff of air. Tall thickets of undergrowth surround the building but thin out toward an unused meadow that was once Albert's pasture.

Grace and Albert Jordan lived up the road a little farther on the left in a simple but almost modern home complete with telephone, hot water, bathroom, running water and indoor washing machine. Their house burned down many years ago after everyone moved away, but the property is still bare and you can see where the foundation of the house was.

Albert was the heartbeat of the creek community not only because he ran the sawmill that supplied necessary winter wood, but also raised milk cows that provided fresh milk to everyone.

He was the mild-mannered preacher at the small 12-member SDA church across the road from his house and was our lifesaver many times when we needed emergency help. They adopted two little boys named Randy and Roger who studied in grandma's little schoolroom.

Gracie would rush to help when we got sick and showed us how to treat our infected chigger and tick bites. She helped us make butter and homemade ice cream. Albert showed me how to properly chop wood so it would fit into the cook stove and how to bank the heating stove at bedtime so it would last all night.

One time I ran to get Albert in the middle of the night when I thought our house was on fire. I'm sure he recounted that experience with a good laugh because the "fire" was only a bunch of lightening bugs Sandra and I had captured that evening.

The last house in the horseshoe of Carver Creek at that time would later become our second house. It was located on a small hill on the right and included five acres of land overlooking Albert's pasture and the creek. We will talk about that experience in the chapter, The House On The Hill.

Here I will interject that when Sandra and I went back to the creek some 30 years later, Tommy Wake was living on our old property in a nice modern mobile home.

He allowed us to explore the property if we promised to close the gate and not let the cows out. Sandra was especially thrilled to meet Tommy again and they chatted about old times for several minutes before we went on our way.

Standing there looking over the hillside, we were awed by the beauty of it all. When we lived there, it took so much just to survive that we didn't see beyond our childhood vision of hard work and a very demanding grandmother.

Today the outline of grandma's garden is still there. The pasture where I said a heartbreaking goodbye to my horse, Princess, is still smooth and green. The lay of the land has not changed much. There is a peaceful tranquility not felt in yesteryear!

This is the end of our Walkabout, but the road does continue to where it crosses the creek again. The only family we remember who lived on the other side of the creek was the Reynard family. A young man lived there who became a frequent guest at our house on the hill.

Norman Reynard was tall, good looking and oh-so polite. He had only one arm due to an accident earlier in life but there was nothing he couldn't do or lift! Norman lived with his parents and helped take care of their farm.

Grandma said Norman had eyes for me. I didn't know what she meant, but I could count on Norman to show up whenever there was heavy work to be done. Many times I would look up to find Norman at my side to offer a helping hand. He was sweet and kind and serious like me. Norman never did anything to make me feel uncomfortable.

Norman was in his early 30's and handicapped so I'm sure he wouldn't have minded taking a sweet teenage wife. Grandma wouldn't have cared if I was 14 or 41 if she thought she could gain a son-in-law to help take care of her too!

But, I thought only of protecting Sandra and finding my mother someday. Anyone I had ever loved had always been left behind.

In the end, Norman drowned trying to cross Carver Creek on his John Deere tractor after a big storm.

*Our first house on Carver Creek many years later.*
*We had no electricity or running water.*
*We bathed in the creek that ran behind the house.*
*Sandra and I were often cold and hungry.*

# Chapter 9

## The House On The Hill

After a winter in David's House (photo on page 42), Albert showed grandma a better place to live a bit farther up the road. I believe he had made a deal with Mr. Wake for us to live there in exchange for grandma's teaching services.

Unlike David's House, this house we named, The House On The Hill, had glass in the windows, a couple of electric lights and one sink of running cold water. Albert and Gracie always kept a watchful eye on us and always offered helping hands.

The edge of the Missouri woods surrounded all three sides of our property on the hill. Any wild animals native to that part of the country traveled in very close proximity to our house.

We often heard the howling of wolves in the night and the mournful baying of Jimmy's hound dogs chasing rabbits. We imagined glowing eyes peering into our bedroom window, and we often heard the soft patter of raccoons, possums and unidentifiable wild animals close to the house.

Standing at our rickety old front door, we could look down the hill to Albert's cow pasture and the sparkling little spring that ran along the edge of the fence. On the other side of his pasture was Carver Creek hidden along the tree line. Beyond the creek was a ridge of Missouri mountains. We always watched for the sun to disappear behind the ridge on Friday evenings signaling the beginning of the Sabbath.

At the bottom of our driveway was our mailbox struggling to remain upright beside the dusty road that Johnny the mailman knew as Rural Route 3. You could see and hear anyone driving up our rocky two-lane driveway because it always put such a strain on the engine to come bumping over the large rocks that protruded from the ground. When it rained a lot, our car got stuck in the muddy ruts, and in the winter we would slip down sideways.

Grandma's garden was located about halfway down and to the left of the driveway. It was surrounded by an old wire fence that was pulled completely down in spots by high weeds and small trees. She must have worked about an acre of land, but it seemed much larger than that to Sandy and me on long hot summer days.

The outside of the house was unevenly wrapped with cheap brown roofing material. Windows had strips of plastic blowing off from the previous winter. Cement steps led to a 4-foot by 4-foot porch and the splinter-like front door that was too old for a lock. The living room walls were bare sheetrock panels covered with splotches of white.

A flea infested couch was shared by the dogs and cats and served as grandma's bed at night. The hub of the living room was the pot-bellied wood stove that needed slabs of wood every half-hour or so during the winter and dominated the living room in the summertime.

Someone had left an age-worn upright piano in a corner of the living room. The ivory on each key had turned brown or had broken off leaving a sticky residue.

The piano leaned forward like it would fall on its face at any moment. I learned to play on this piano by putting pennies on the knuckles of each finger as I practiced.

I sat on an old can for a piano stool and by the time I was 14, I was playing the piano for the little Seventh-day Adventist church that was located between Albert's house and our hill.

The kitchen consisted of plank shelves on one wall and a wood-burning cooking stove on the other side. Sheets of fireproof material hung behind each stove to keep the walls from catching on fire.

An old white icebox sat next to the plank shelves, but grandma never cleaned it out so the food was usually all covered with hairy green mold. The freezer contained nothing but undefrosted ice and buttons of homemade butter.

The only sink in the house was wedged in front of the kitchen window that looked out into the back yard. It sat between boxes of dishes grandma never unpacked and an old unused electric stove. A small kitchen closet with a tiny ladder leading to the attic was on the adjoining wall next to the electric stove.

Dishes were done, hair washed (with bars of soap) and baths were taken in pans of cold water. The laundry was still done on scrub boards outside in the front yard – summer and winter!

Every morning grandma or I would build a tiny little fire in the firebox inside the cookstove and wait until the stove top was hot enough for cooking, but not too hot to burn the food. Instead of cornmeal mush or oatmeal, grandma could now make tomato gravy and hot biscuits.

The biscuits always had the sharp taste of too much baking powder and the tomato gravy had to be checked closely for the occasional large green worm someone had missed in the canning process. I always left a small amount of food on my plate so I could pretend that all the worms were in that part of the plate.

Those shelves along the wall of the kitchen were packed with jars of flour, macaroni, rice, cornmeal and beans and, if you looked closely, all in a slow perpetual motion of white worms and weevils. Grandma also kept a few quart jars of vegetables on these shelves, but most of the garden food for winter was stored in the cellar.

The odor of cat feces in the winter and baskets of over-ripe fruit and vegetables in the summertime was powerful, but we got used to it after awhile.

We would unconsciously reach down and brush the fleas from our ankles when we entered the house but they still ate at our legs all summer. Sandra and I never got used to pulling big fat ticks from each other. We would scream and dance around not sure what to do with the tick and wondering if we had left his head behind!

By the time we moved to the house on the hill, we had adjusted to the drastic change in our environment. By now, we had gotten to know Johnny the mailman and to watch for the tiny dust trail that would signal his car coming down the road. Taking a break from the garden, we would run to the rusty old mailbox, our bare feet jumping up and down with anticipation of a letter from grandpa.

Grandpa wrote often and sent news of our cousins. We also took turns taking the mail to an old lady who lived down the hill at the back of our house. We don't remember why Mrs. Butler lived all alone or how she managed to stay alive, but she counted on us to bring her mail every day (whether she got mail or not). She paid us 25 cents a week.

What Sandra and I liked most about the house on the hill was the attic where we could play and hide our personal belongings from grandma. We placed pieces of wood between the rafters and we never once fell through!

We climbed into the attic on a little ladder grandpa made for us in the closet. There we had blankets to keep us warm and used a work light that grandpa made for us during one of his rare visits.

Grandpa knew the attic was our only escape when grandma became enraged, wild and unrestrained with her terrible unbridled temper. It was a quiet place where Sandra could nurse her wounds or I could write in my diary.

In the safe confines of the attic we hid what few old toys and dolls we had. We could always discover a new nest of tiny, pink wiggly baby mice to play with, or we watched quietly when mother birds flew in to feed their squawking baby birds.

I had a little space in the attic where I could finally hide my diary from grandma and keep my solitary pen and pieces of paper. Later, we hid letters from grandpa and our cousins up there but we were devastated when the mice eventually chewed them to shreds.

I think the dusty angels must have protected my five-year diary, the resource for this book 43 years later!

The magnificent foothills of the beautiful Ozark Mountains didn't seem so imposing now. The meadow for Albert's lazy cows changed colors with the seasons, but always lay quiet and peaceful at the foot of our hill.

To the north side of our house, a couple fruit trees provided thick thorny branches that grandma tore off and used to whip us with. The fresh-looking fruit was always full of worms. Just beyond the fruit trees was a small pasture for Princess, my faithful but spirited horse and Beulah the milk goat we got from Vernon. They shared a small barn where I milked Beulah morning and night.

Albert found Princess, a beautiful brown colt with large baby eyes lying in a muddy barnyard with a broken leg. He brought the Tennessee Walker to me and I nursed her back to health. Albert showed me what to feed her and he supplied medicine and shots when she needed it. I had to carry buckets of water to her, and I was always trying to rebuild the old wire fence that never kept either the horse or goat contained.

A few years later it would almost gave Albert a heart attack to see me riding Princess bareback as she galloped wildly down the road.

Behind the house were two small wooden sheds and the "two-seater" outhouse. We called the larger shed the "Girls Ranch." It didn't matter that the chickens and geese roosted secure from foxes at night under the Girls Ranch; we enjoyed sleeping out there away from grandma when we could. The building had a tin roof and when it rained, nothing else mattered in the world because you couldn't hear anything except the loud clatter of the rain.

The outhouse sat on the edge of a hill and shook so badly when we stepped inside, we feared it would slide out from under us every time we sat down on the holes that were too large for our tiny bodies. The dry gray boards had large gaps that were always alive with bugs and spiders. Of course the odor was typical of an outhouse with its putrid rank and masses of wiggly worms deep inside, but the Sears catalog pages used for toilet paper was better then the leaves in the woods we had been using.

If we didn't wake to the faraway sound of grandma's persistent voice calling us from the garden, we would waken to the early morning birdcalls of the mourning doves and bobwhites next to our bedroom window. Sandra and I felt sorry for the bird that kept repeating, "Whip-Poor-Will." We wondered what he had done wrong.

Later, we converted an old back porch into a sleeping room, weather permitting. The screen door was filled with holes that let in the mosquitoes, rain and other bugs. The floor sagged in the center and there was no electric light out there. My little bed was right next to the screen door where I could see the night animals scampering about.

Next to my bed was a trap door that led down into a small underground cellar. It was more like a hole in the ground under the porch, and the steps were too unsteady for grandma to use, so Sandra and I carefully carried the jars of food down the rickety steps and gingerly set them on the thick wooden shelves. There were also piles of sawdust on the dirt cellar floor for the potatoes, turnips and other vegetables from the garden.

I have often imagined those jars of food are still lined up on all those shelves deep underground where our house once stood.

Our house on the hill burned down in a rash of fires along the creek soon after we left. Today all that is left are the cement steps looking strangely out of place under a large tree.

Within a few months of moving to our house on the hill, we were managing quite a menagerie of wild animals and pets. Someone gave us a small cream-colored goat we named Little Jewell. Her horns had been burned or cut off, but it didn't turn out right so she had little stubs between her ears. She liked to butt the dogs and anyone else who got in her way! We especially enjoyed watching Little Jewell butt grandma out of the way while calmly eating the flowers off the lilac bush every year.

The geese would come running with wings spread low when we called, "here geesie, geesie, geesie." Rooster Domino who had spurs like sharp darts and was ruler of the chicken house, always raced ahead of the geese for his share of corn. He especially liked to fly up in Sandra's face and scratch her legs when she wasn't expecting it.

We collected baby animals from the woods all the time. We took in baby possums, baby birds, and baby rattlesnakes (not knowing they were rattlesnakes). Sandra still tells the story of when the possum ate all her baby mice we were "raising" in the same box.

Our cats had kittens on our bed. Beulah had triplet kids (baby goats), and the chickens were always nesting. Sometimes we "set" a hen on a nest of eggs and counted the days for the exact day the eggs would hatch. On hatching day, we would sit and watch the eggs crack open with tiny little peck holes getting bigger and bigger until the shell cracked open enough for the small biddy to hop out.

During the summer, Albert dumped a large pile of wood slabs from his sawmill next to our house. These large chunks of wood had to be split for the wood stove and splintered for the cook stove. Often, I split the wood with grandma's huge dull ax. I think the heavy old ax weighed more than I did. Sandra and I spent long hours on hot summer days splitting the wood, stacking it in the woodshed.

We knew if the woodpile fell over or if grandma couldn't get one stick into the small opening of the cookstove, she would become violently crazed with anger and one of us (usually Sandra) would get slammed with the frying pan, whipped with the sharp metal spatula or slashed with a strong thorny stick from the apple tree.

# Chapter 10

## It Wasn't The Garden of Eden

*Grandma Mascunana*
*works in her garden*

I was racing my horse across Albert's soft green pasture, my long brown hair flying in the wind, my head held tight against her neck and my tummy flat against her back as I hung on to her mane for dear life.

Princess was wild with abandonment, kicking out her hind legs as she ran with her head held high and ears laid flat.

The skies were blue and the air sweet and clear. I was free and light as a feather in the wind.

Suddenly I was falling, falling, falling into a deep chasm toward the faraway voice of an angry woman.

"Linda! Sandra! Are you going to sleep all day? Get up right now before I have to come up there!"

It was grandma calling us from out in the garden. And, it was only 5:00 in the morning.

Scurrying to find something to wear from the pile of clothes in one corner of the room and knowing we had to empty the chamber pot and let the chickens out before we got to the garden, Sandra and I worked fast and furious before grandma had time to stomp into the house with her big stick

Sandra's legs were still red and swollen from the last beating with a board that had a few rusty nails left in it. She limped with pain as she carried the water bucket to the chicken house and slung handfuls of corn to the geese.

I had tried to make a potato poultice for the ugly infections in Sandra's legs and raw wounds on our backs, but we knew if grandma saw the bandages, she would get mad and whack us again and again.

Grandma was in her own little heaven when she was working in her garden but she could not have succeeded without the long, backbreaking, sweltering hours she forced Sandra and me to labor in her garden.

During the previous winter she had poured over the Burpee catalogs for hours at a time deciding what would be ordered in time for the spring thaw.

She planted her garden in accordance with the Farmer's Almanac and in competition with everyone else on the creek, but especially Mr. Westbrook.

If he planted watermelons, she planted cantaloupe. He planted raspberry plants and she planted strawberry plants.

Grandma in her stubbornness would sometimes plant too early or not in sync with the moon's phase to get ahead of someone else, but sure enough, those plantings usually failed to germinate or lagged behind in growth

Mr. Westbrook must have done something right because his garden always produced more than anyone else on the creek and, many years later, his 15-foot tall raspberry bushes had overgrown the old property.

All summer we helped gather vegetables and put them into jars for the winter months. First, we washed the hundreds of quart jars in a big tub of icy cold water our in the yard. Then we watched as the jars were put into hot water on the kitchen cookstove along with the lids to be sterilized.

After carefully filling each jar with hot vegetables we had gleaned from the garden and prepared by hand, and gently wiping the rim of the jar clean, we would screw on the ring to hold the lid in place until it sealed.

We would listen for the Pop or Ping (depending on the size of the jar) that would indicate the jar was officially sealed.

Many summer nights after Sandra and I were in bed, we would count the little pop or ping of the seals. If one did not seal by morning, we stood a good chance of a hard whipping from grandma. She would blame us for not washing the jars good enough or not cleaning the rim before we set the lid.

The garden season would start when the spring mornings were still dark and cold. Our work would not be completed until the ground was frozen and winter's snow was spitting in our faces. As we finally picked the last green bean and collected the final basket of tomatoes, grandma would continue trying to dig up one last potato until her shovel could no longer break into the frozen ground.

When construction of the St. Louis Arch dominated that city from 1963 to1967, grandma's garden dominated our lives. When teenagers in St. Louis were river rafting and dancing to the Beatles in the summertime, we would be summoned to the garden before daybreak and work wearily until the last light of day. We would fall into bed stopping only long enough for a bedtime prayer. (Sandra didn't pray if grandma wasn't looking.)

One year my diary records the garden season like this.

April 11, "We planted strawberry plants today."
April 19, "Everyone came and we plowed and planted potatoes."
April 21, "We planted peas and corn."
May 16, "We planted tomato plants all day."
May 31, "We planted cane in the field today."
June 24, "I picked raspberries today."
July 19, "Everyone worked in the cane patch today."
August 4, "We got bushels of peaches to can."
August 16, "We canned the last of the peaches."

August 18, "This morning we canned corn. Worms too!"

August 19, "We canned soup mix all day."

September 6, "We picked and shelled peas all day."

August 20, "We shelled lima beans all day and canned them all night."

September 21, "We canned pears today."

September 26, "We dug potatoes at Westbrook's all day."

September 30, "We cut and got all the cane in the barn today."

October 11, "We picked up walnuts all day."

October 18, "We dug up our potatoes today."

October 21, "We dug up peanuts all day. Lloyd is going to boil them for us."

October 22, "Got last of peppers and green tomatoes."

November 23, "We got a bushel of turnips for 50 cents."

In the fall, we helped dig potatoes from the garden and picked up walnuts from under the trees. The barn would be stacked with bales of hay for the goats and Princess. Firewood was stacked neatly in the woodshed and another pile next to the front door. Plastic was tacked to the windows and the back bedrooms were closed off. Wood boxes were filled with kindling to start a morning fire in the big living room stove and in the kitchen wood stove.

By the time winter's blast closed the roads and our little school, we knew it would be months before we could visit our friends along the creek. I would have to get up early every morning and push my way through snowdrifts to milk the goat. The firewood would be under mounds of frozen snow. Water buckets would be heavy with ice.

There would be no mail from grandpa or his family. Christmas would come and go without fanfare.

It would be a long, cold winter living with an angry old woman who often beat us nearly to death for no reason, and who never once said, I love you.

# Chapter 11

## Sanctuary in the Attic

Sandra and I shared the private mystery of why we lived with grandma and what happened to our family, but we didn't openly share our opinion of grandma. Sandra suffered physically far more than I did because she stood up to grandma and didn't let grandma control or crush her strong free spirit.

"I not do!" were her first words to grandma when taken from the orphanage and placed in grandma's care. Later, she would scurry under the kitchen table out of grandma's reach or quickly climb into the attic where grandma couldn't follow.

My strength was spent in a never-ending struggle to take care of everyone and keep grandma in a good mood so she wouldn't hurt us. I was constantly torn between trying to be good for grandma, and not hating her when she was so hurtful. In turn, Sandra felt like I had abandoned her when I was obedient, and grandma often used my loyalty to her advantage.

Grandpa knew that we desperately needed his love and support. After the first bitter winter, he sent large packages of toys and pretty clothes to try and make up for his long absences. He never knew that we didn't get to keep the gifts from him and his family.

Shouting with delight and lugging the brown paper-wrapped boxes up the hill from the mailbox, Sandra and I would excitedly tear them open.

But the merriment would quickly fade, as grandma took the presents from our hands saying we needed to share with, "those less fortunate."

Once in a while, we would find some little leftover gift and hide it in the attic. The diary used for this story was one of those presents – a Christmas gift from George and Rose Marie Mascunana that was rescued from grandma's "less fortunate box" and kept hidden in the attic until grandma forgot about it.

We rarely saw our Christmas gifts from grandpa's family after we opened the packages. We didn't get to wear the pretty clothes or keep the precious toys. Candy disappeared and food was given away.

Grandma ignored our birthdays too. When Barbie Dolls were the rage for all the girls, and when young boys were getting brand-new 3-speed bikes for their birthday, our birthdays slipped by unannounced and uncelebrated. Sandra and I would sometimes quietly slip gifts to each other, but only things grandma wouldn't notice.

Sandra's birthday is June 15. On her birthday in 1964 I wrote, *"Grandma took Nelda to town. We stayed with her kids."* On another year it says, *"We cleaned the kitchen and living room today."*

My birthday was incorrectly thought to be on September 3, but in Missouri it didn't matter. The only birthday mentioned is on my 15th birthday when grandma took me to town and let me pick out something. I selected some barrettes for my hair not knowing she had a scheming reason for this unusual bit of kindness.

Grandma was in trouble and she wanted me beholding to her because she was about to use me in her deceiving way to cover some bad tracks.

Grandma was a gossip and a troublemaker who hid her wrongs under the umbrella of religion. She often used me as her peacemaker

Our neighbors would often get into arguments at our house, screaming at grandma and accusing her of lying and causing trouble between people. The ladies would usually leave in tears - furious but unable to break her spirit. I would write little notes in my diary about problems with grandma, but always careful to make grandma look good because I knew she would read my diary whenever she could.

The birthday trip was noted carefully in my diary, but the event made life harder for me because Sandra always said that I got favorable treatment, and this seemed to prove her point.

Years later I would discover that my birthday is really September 6, but I have continued with the traditional September 3 because of the confusion the change caused.

In spite of the abuse and unloving spirit we suffered at grandma's hands, Sandra and I always remembered grandma on Mother's Day with homemade gifts we thought she would like and we always presented her with thoughtful gifts on her birthday, August 26.

So, as a young teenager, I became the parent figure although not without some scorn and ridicule from Sandra. When we would get into a sisterly argument, Sandra would holler at me, "I hate you!" Grandma would smack Sandra sharply in the face and order her to apologize to me. Feigning an apology in order to avoid a brutal beating, Sandra would have the last word when grandma left the room. "I still hate you," she would whisper.

I knew Sandra didn't hate me. She was a battered child. She had no outlet for the awful frustration, unspeakable pain and mental anguish grandma caused her. Her mother and father abandoned her before she was old enough to remember them. Grandma put disturbing thoughts into her head about her parents. She felt like her mother must hate her and her father didn't want to claim her!

To Sandra, it did look like I was "grandma's favorite" because my response to losing my mother was to be good so she would come back. But the effect of trying to make everyone happy and feeling the loss of everyone I loved, would eventually take its toll on my health.

# Chapter 12

## *Deceptively Legal*

When I was eleven years old, we traveled by car from Missouri to Sebring, Florida to be formally adopted. Grandpa would soon turn 65 and they wanted to claim us on his Social Security. One of the most deceitful deeds grandma did was when she went to court to adopt us. Grandma lied to the court and said she had not heard from our parents since she got us, when in fact she was hiding us from both our parents and was in contact with our father on a regular basis.

Apparently the state of New York was not informed of this action because years earlier it had refused to give us over to her as she was considered by the state of New York to be unstable!

But nevertheless, in June of 1962, our last name was legally changed from Brantley to Mascunana.

The Brantley family never recognized this adoption. If so, our dad would now be our brother and all our aunts and uncles would be our siblings! They all remained as we had known them, "Aunt Tina, Uncle Bill, Uncle George Jr. and Daddy."

The Mascunana family was totally confused. But, worst of all, this mean-tempered giant of a woman who had destroyed any chance of a normal life for us, was now our legal mother!

The chastisement and maltreatment took on new meaning. We felt trapped, unloved and unwanted. It seemed we would never escape her ruthless brutality. She was shameless in her domination over us. She refused to let us mention our mother's name again. My few attempts to contact relatives in New York City were met with unrestrained horror and savage beatings.

When our pain was too intense after a bad day with grandma, we often took refuge in the dark corners of the attic surrounded by spider webs and mice nests. Our bodies were often broken and bleeding. Our minds cloudy with slow burning pain.

Sometimes I would find Sandra coiled way back in the edges of the attic, hugging her knees and bowing her head in defeat. She would be almost as angry at me as she was at grandma. She thought I could take her and run away, but we had no place to go and I thought there was no one left who cared. I wondered how long I must wait for the day I could resume the search for our mother. A pursuit I knew would never end until I found her and the reason why she left.

# Chapter 13

## "A Family Friend"

On July 4, 1965, when I was 14 years old, I straightened up from the endless chopping at the dry hard garden soil. The hoe was dull, the handle broken and full of splinters. My tired back ached with a dull throbbing that I knew would continue for many hours.

I noticed a little trail of dust off in the distance on the road and wondered who would be coming down Carver Creek Road at this time of day. Johnny had already stopped by and left our mail. Nothing from grandpa. Maybe tomorrow.

Hoping grandma wouldn't notice my slacking, I leaned on the fence post as I felt a strangeness come over me. My heart seemed to be skipping beats and my stomach was doing flip-flops. The car was slowing. A man was waving. It was turning into our driveway!

Walking slowly to the garden gate, I paused and peered at a familiar face. The man smiled a smile that looked just like mine! His face was warm with tenderness and brown from hours of fishing at sea.

Needing no introduction, I stepped cautiously closer and said, "Hello Daddy."

It was our dad!

Grandma didn't seem surprised to see her son, but Sandra and I were wild with excitement! All these years we had waited and I had not forgotten our mother's last words. *"Wait for me. Your Daddy or I will come for you."*

"How long are you staying? Did you come for us? Will you take us swimming? How did you find us?"

Daddy had come to offer us a nice home with a sweet stepmother and three sisters, two of whom were twins!

Grandma let him drive us to town for commodities and we went swimming and had a picnic, but a few days after his sudden arrival, grandma shipped me off to the only church-related summer camp I ever attended.

I was devastated at not being able to stay with my dad! For two glorious days we had taken daddy everywhere, hanging on to his arms and holding his hand. We showered him with hugs and kisses, much to grandma's chagrin.

At first, grandma was embarrassed by daddy's smoking and tried to present this chain-smoking stranger as, "a family friend," but Sandra quickly squelched that by announcing to everyone that this was her daddy and he had come to take her home!

At camp I became ill with homesickness and sick at heart to think daddy might be gone when I got back! How my arms ached for his touch and my head hurt with anxious worry!

But I had no choice. My diary reflects that I stayed busy getting honors in birds, reptiles, and swimming.

*"We watched the sun go down around a campfire and took a long walk in the woods,"* I faithfully recorded every day!

I got a letter from grandma while I was at camp. She said they had canned 91 quarts of green beans. I wrote in my diary, *"At home I guess they are all having a family reunion. Boy, would I like to be at home."*

When the SDA Conference pastor finally brought me home two weeks later, I was so brown that everybody laughed and called me an Indian. I now looked like a miniature of my dad!

I returned home on July 25 at 7:00 p.m., and flew into my daddy's arms. We spent the next week canning tomatoes, picking corn and snapping bushels of green beans.

On his last day there, Daddy stepped out his cigarette on the ground and said, "Let's go to church." He attended the weekly prayer meeting service with me, but by then, we knew that he wouldn't be taking us with him. Sandra was bitterly heartbroken. I was confused and felt responsible for not being able to make it right.

On August 4, 1965, I wrote,
*Dear Diary...*

*"Elder Sharpe had prayer meeting. We went swimming with Daddy.*
*HE LEFT TODAY!"*

Grandma had legal control now, and there was nothing he could do. He left us for the last time, and he never came to see us again.

# Chapter 14

## _Little Girl Mother_

My five-year Missouri diary tells the story of a hardworking, serious, mature teenager who thought a good day was getting the chores done, the house clean, bread in the oven and wash on the clothesline by 9 a.m.

This was when clothes were still scrubbed on a scrub board in a tub of cold water in the front yard. Bread was cooked in a woodstove oven that needed a perfectly controlled fire to bake the bread to a golden brown, and the chores included milking the goat and watering the chickens, geese, goats and horse with buckets of water carried from the house.

The daily entries in my diary when I was 13 look like this:

"Went to Ironton for commodities. Got frostbitten on the way there."

"Got up at 6:30 and had all our work done before we went to school."

"Lilly came over and we mopped our floors and got all our wash done."

"Sandra was sick today, so I did the washing and I had a headache."

"I stayed home from school with Sandra."

"Grandma has been getting mad all day, but she was ok after prayer meeting."

"I did the cooking today so we wouldn't have so much to do tomorrow."

"We did our washing today. After we got back from Esteys, we did the ironing."

"I got all the weeds out of the garden except corn, beans and potatoes."

"My stomach hurt all day, but I washed and ironed."

"I cleaned grandma's room, mopped the floors and cleaned the yard."

"I washed clothes today while grandma went to town."

"I made eight loaves of bread and two pans of rolls today."

"It was below freezing all day but I washed, and the clothesline fell down twice."

"I stayed up until 3:30 a.m. sewing."

To celebrate becoming a teenager the summer of 1964, I planted my own little flower garden behind the Ranch House. I chipped away at the brick-hard ground with a heavy old railroad pick for many days until my hands were red with blisters. Then I carefully broke up the chunks of soil and smoothed out a little square plot. Carefully placing a tiny flower seed into each hole and tenderly watering the soil every day, I watched for the tiny green sprouts to peek from the earth.

I was rewarded with a plant from every seed and within a few weeks I picked summer flowers unlike anyone on the creek had ever seen! That summer I enjoyed the first flower garden of my life. Every few days I refreshed the kitchen table with another bunch of my stunningly colorful flowers.

I was a survivor! I had become a good cook. I sewed clothes and made quilts on grandma's old pedal pushing Singer sewing machine. Every tire on the old Oldsmobile had been changed several times even though I had to jump on the tire tool to loosen the bolts. Princess was contained in the pasture after the fences got mended with new posts and strong wire (and Albert's help). The bags of feed weighed more than I did as I heaved the burly bags into the barn (with Norman's help). Princess was never thirsty for fresh water. I cooked, sewed, cleaned, canned food and tried to study from any book I could find.

One day we were happily surprised when a young couple from St. Louis moved down to the property in the woods next to ours. Charlie and Eva Allen and their two little boys, Mark and

David, soon became close friends, and we visited back and forth every day.

Eva was especially nice to me and helped me understand the changes in my body. She showed me different ways to fix my hair and wear my drabby dresses. She and Charlie took me to the doctor visits when I lost weight and became weak and faint.

Eva didn't get along well with grandma, and that caused me great distress. Eventually Eva refused to come to our house when grandma was present. My diary often reflected the hurt and pain of her avoidance by the oft-repeated phrase, *"Eva didn't come over today."* Eva finally left the creek and my life completely. She was a special friend that I missed for a long time.

For a couple years, we also provided a foster home to a mentally retarded teenager named Davey. I believe grandma expected to use Davey to help with the heavy garden work and chores, but he was more trouble than help. He didn't follow directions and got into heated arguments with Sandra. I was often the peacemaker when he got grandma riled up and bickered with Sandra.

Once when grandma was gone for a few days to a church campmeeting, I woke up in the middle of the night to find Davey standing over me with the kitchen butcher knife. In a few more seconds he would have slashed or stabbed me. Grandma did nothing in response to my terrified telephone call for her help, but after that I hid all the knives and watched Davey very carefully.

# Chapter 15

## Day Is Dying In The West

"*I had all the work done and I would have had the chores done before sundown, but I couldn't find my horse!*"

There are about forty-eight Fridays in a year, and every Friday for five years, I indicated with a note in my diary if we were ready to herald in the Sabbath at the moment of sundown every Friday evening.

Occasionally the wood wasn't in yet or grandma wasn't home from town, but most of the time I had everything as clean as I could get it, Sabbath dinner cooked, church clothes laid out and a list of songs I would play for tomorrow's church service ready for Albert.

As the sun set behind the mountain ridge in the western sky, grandma would open one of Ellen G. White's books for worship and I would sigh with relief and sit at the old upright piano to play, "Day Is Dying In the West." Every Seventh-day Adventist knows the words to that traditional Friday sunset song.

> *Day is dying in the west.*
> *Heaven is touching earth with rest.*
> *Wait and worship while the night*
> *Sets the evening lamps alight*
> *Through all the sky.*

The website to hear the piano music to this song almost as I played it in Missouri every Friday night is found at: www. digitalhymnal.org

On Saturdays we walked down the hill and through the pasture to the little white church/schoolhouse for church services. There were only about ten pews in the brick building and sometimes only a half-dozen people attended.

More of the creek people attended church when they knew Sandra and I were going to sing for special music. Our voices harmonized very well, but Sandra hated singing about Jesus. She didn't believe that Jesus was a very nice person to make her life so hard and to have taken away her mother and daddy.

Sandra often protested to me (not grandma) and threatened to sing the words, "Jesus Hates Me" instead of "Jesus Loves Me". I always poked her in the ribs at that point and she knew what I meant. She never let me down, but I never knew for sure if she was going to try and pull that off.

Grandma rarely let us have a rest from the backbreaking garden work or endless housework and chores. But, once in a while we were allowed to go on a daytrip to St. Louis with a neighbor or to ride along with someone who was going into Ironton for supplies. Most of the time, she went on those trips and left us alone to do the chores.

Wednesday afternoons we drove to Annapolis for piano lessons if grandma felt like it and the creeks weren't up.

My diary shows that we missed more times than we went, but our music teacher, Mrs. Whitledge, must have known that those priceless moments with her were the happiest of my hard life. She quickly moved me up to a grade three piano book and she gave me a miniature accordion.

My diary reflects that once we went to St. Louis with Charlie and Eva to help them move the rest of their things to the creek. We stayed about a week and during the time we were there I wrote, *"I just love it here. It is so much fun here"* even though we spent most of that time helping them pack and scrub down their house.

Another time I wrote that Albert had gone to St. Louis while it was raining. I noted that the creek was rising and I was afraid he couldn't get across when he got back that night. The next day I wrote that Vernon had pulled his car across the creek with his truck!

I wrote about the little things like how much Mr. Wake sold a piece of property for (11 acres for $414.00), if one of our tires was

66

going bad or if someone was mad at grandma. I noted when one of Albert's cows had a calf, when the bugs were eating the tomato plants and when Mr. Westbrook made a change in his garden. I kept track of people grandma took to town and who was not feeling well. Daily weather conditions were noted carefully in my diary.

Two events happened on October 20, 1965 that are recorded in my very old diary. I have written, *"We saw a jet flame and fall"* and, on the same day I have the word, *"Earthquake"* circled with uneven lines.

A quick Internet search now produces information on those two events.

On October 20, 1965 there was an earthquake in eastern Missouri that affected 160,000 square miles. On that same date at 7:30 p.m., a jet crashed in Green City, Missouri. The cause is listed as an incorrect weather forecast.

I was already a budding news reporter even though I had no way to know that about 30 years later I would become a newspaper correspondent in my town of Berrien Springs, Michigan.

# Chapter 16

## *School on a Good Day*

School was grandma's little one-room schoolhouse where we had one book per subject for all the students in the room. There was no study hall, PE or gym. We had no school assembly, no senior class, and no proms, pep rallies, clubs or sports. I took the same tests year after year when I should have been in grades 8-12.

One day in 1963, grandma told us that the president of the United States had been shot and killed. We didn't know who the president was!

Grandma was officially a teacher for the Missouri Conference of Seventh-day Adventists. Many days grandma didn't open school for one reason or another, but if she did, I often stayed home to clean, cook, wash clothes or work in the garden - alone.

The times I did walk down the hill to the tiny classroom, I usually spent my time helping the students with their papers or giving the church-required tests to the younger students.

Grandma was pleased when I would take her place in the classroom while she took someone to get commodities or went into town for one reason or another.

She was stricter about our clothing and our playtime than she was about our education. When girls my age were wearing bell-bottom pants and platform shoes, I wore long dresses that had to cover my knees, and I went barefoot most of the time. Shoes were saved for church or a special trip to town.

Blue jeans, pants, sleeveless dresses and bathing suits were never allowed. Grandma read from the Ellen G. White Books where it said that dressing like this was unholy and attracted too much attention to our bodies.

When teenagers in the 60's were dancing to, "The Twist", "Rock-N-Roll", "The Stroll", "The Mashed Potato" and "The Swim," we were told that dancing came from the devil and to avoid any forms of dancing like the plague.

When transistor radios were shaping the medium of teenage music in the 60's, my only source of radio was when I would sneak out to the car and listen to the news on KMOX Radio out of St. Louis.

"Pope Paul was in New York today," I noted in my diary on October 5, 1965. I wasn't supposed to be listening to the car radio, so I couldn't talk about this news to anyone in the house.

I couldn't tell anyone about the 31st Anniversary of President and Mrs. Johnson on November 17, 1965 when I heard that tidbit on the news that day, but I wrote about it in my diary.

Grandma had intense beliefs about music too. When kids were paying 89 cents for the first two-song 45-RPM records, the only music we heard was in church or when the mountain folk would gather around Jimmy Jordan playing his fiddle on a Saturday night.

When teenagers were harmonizing and dancing to Ricky Nelson's, "Hello Mary Lou" and "Traveling Man," Sandra and I were singing comfort songs to elderly shut-ins.

Our voices blended as one when we sang, "Jesus Loves The Little Children of the World" and "Amazing Grace" to the old people. We sang for local funerals, in nursing homes, and a few times, we sang on a radio show hosted by Mr. Westbrook.

# Chapter 17

## A Promise Broken

I was almost 16 and without formal schooling, but I was making good grades with home study courses. I was cooking, washing and cleaning and teaching most every day. I attended prayer meeting every Wednesday night, took piano lessons every Tuesday and played the piano at church every Saturday.

Some of the folks noticed that I was looking pale and thin. When I fainted after playing the opening song for church one Sabbath, grandma was forced to admit I was not well. Charlie and Eva drove me to the doctor in Fredericktown – 32 miles away.

The doctor said my stomachaches were from nerves, my backaches were caused from the wagon injury, and that I had severe anemia. He gave me a B12 shot and ordered grandma to bring me back every month for additional injections. At 14 years, my weight was less than 80 pounds.

My diary is still void of emotion, but I use small symbols that alert me to the fact that I know grandma is reading it. I find entries erased and grandma's handwriting changing some words. At least I still have the diary. I worry that she will destroy it.

I suspect grandma is having trouble with some of the parents and that the conference is not pleased with her work.

Grandma had promised me that as long as I completed all the home study lessons, I could stay at home with Sandra and keep our pets and my precious horse Princess. But something was amiss and I could feel it near the end of 1965.

On November 14, 1965 I wrote, *"Today I gave Little Jewell away. I miss her more than anything."*

During the summer we had sold Beulah and her kids for $35.00.

Charlie Allen had taken most of our chickens, and our favorite dog, Goldie, had been taken to St. Louis and given away.

*"Something is wrong,"* I record in my diary on December 12, 1965.

On January 6, 1966, I receive a letter from Carolyn Westbrook (David's wife) inviting me to come and live with them in Gentry, Arkansas and attend the SDA Academy there.

I did not reply.

I was keeping my end of the bargain that grandma made with me.

Did I suspect that grandma would not keep hers?

On January 8, Carolyn called grandma on Albert's phone.

*"She told grandma about a house,"* I note without comment in my diary.

In my heart I know our days in Missouri are nearing the end. After six years in these mountains, I don't want to leave the only place I now call home. I have endured and learned to love the simple people of Carver Creek. I am at peace with the majestic mountains. We can exist in this backwoods wonderland. No one else can ride my faithful horse like I do as she gallops wildly down the rocky, dusty road.

I am the only one who can play the Doxology at church. The cellar is full of winter's food, and the barn is packed with fresh sweet hay. The firewood is ready for the winter stoves.

On January 9, everyone leaves for Gentry, Arkansas leaving me alone to do the chores.

*"At 4:30 today Esther and Cindy went with Grandma and Sandra to Arkansas."* I knew this trip was about my life but I was left behind to do the chores.

To make matters worse, grandma had asked Vernon and Juanita to stay the night with me. How could she NOT know about that man? I slept with a large butcher knife under my pillow that night.

Everyone returned late on January 10 and, according to meticulous notes in my diary, the next day I started packing.

On January 11, I simply wrote, *"Grandma went to town. I got my room packed."*

For January 14, there is the simple word, **"Princess"** and the unwritten heavy feeling of unspeakable pain.

That night I had walked Princess to Albert's pasture knowing that Albert would have to put her down. Tears flowed between horse and master. Princess knew my heart was breaking. For the first time in her life, she stood quietly next to me. She rubbed her nose up and down against my cheek as I wept and held her tight. I knew nothing in my life would ever hurt this badly again. It was time for my life to start anew and hers to end.

No one asked, and I told no one what I had done with Princess.

On January 15, we packed the truck.

On January 16 I write simply,

**Dear Diary...***"This morning grandma decided not to leave until tonight and tonight she decided to leave in the morning."*

# Chapter 18

## A Time to Spread My Wings

We left Missouri when I was almost 17 years old and grandma was feeling the heat for my lack of education.

Before sunrise on January 17, 1966 we bumped down our rocky driveway for the last time. It was 22 degrees and the car had no heat. Shivering from the cold and exhausted from the events of the last few weeks, I fell into a fitful sleep and dreamed that Princess was back in her stall munching on sweet hay and I was building a warm fire in the kitchen cookstove for breakfast.

We made the 345-mile trip by 9 p.m. that night. Carolyn Westbrook, true to her word, had found us a house, but someone had forgotten to have the electric turned on so the house was dark and cold when we finally arrived. We hurried to get the car empty and slept on the floor the first night there.

The following morning I registered for school at Ozark Academy. Sandra would attend the elementary school on the same campus.

Within a few weeks of the winter semester, I had passed the required tests to enter the 9th grade. After a couple months of flute lessons every Tuesday afternoon, I was playing, "Bonanza" in the school band.

I quickly became aware of the fast changing time of the 60's. I learned about the Camelot years, the Vietnam War and America's first spacewalk.

Grandma soon had me employed in a small nursing home where I worked the night shift from 11 p.m. to 7 a.m.

I'm not sure why she thought it was so important for me to take on a job, but even though my diary indicates I was having terrible stomachaches, my back and legs hurt much of the time and I was often extremely sleepy and very tired, I never missed a day of school or a night shift of work.

Within a few months, I was passing medicines in the nursing home and supervising the evening shift in the kitchen without formal certification of any kind for the job.

I loved the challenges of real schoolwork, making friends with girls (and boys!) my age, going to town on my own and, on Saturday, playing the piano for a roomful of little kids at church.

My diary written while at Ozark Academy is filled with busy but exciting times of hard work and a fast paced school schedule. I excelled in English, Biology, Math, Bible, Typing and History at the Academy and still finished the home study courses I had started in Missouri.

I kept grandma's checkbook up to date and paid bills grandma left unpaid in Missouri. I was still changing flat tires and repairing things that were broken in the house.

One day was so important to me that I wrote boldly in my usual brief entry. *"Today I bought a pretty white dress."* My first shopping spree!

Driving the car to Gentry with my new official drivers license, I went shopping alone. Browsing the shopping center, my mind was overwhelmed with so many choices! Should I get this for Sandra? Would grandma like me to get her that? Ohhh, grandpa would really like this for his birthday!

But, when I saw a little white dress just my size hanging at the end of the aisle, my heart nearly stopped beating and I could hardly breathe! It was so dainty and beautiful with a scalloped neckline and softly gathered shirt. The flowing long sleeves had a small shiny button on each cuff and someone had embroidered little flowers all over the front of the angelic dress.

A pleasant lady asked if I would like to try it on as she showed me the door to the dressing room. I was afraid it would vanish in my hands as I stepped into the soft smooth material and the nice lady zipped up the back.

It fit around my tiny waist instantly and covered my little bra just right. The flowing skirt was shorter than I was used to covering the top edge of my knees, but the woman helping me said it was just right and made me look like an angel.

Not sure if I would get in trouble for making such a large purchase that would take all the money I had saved for this occasion, I excitedly called grandma on the phone to ask if I could have the dress. She approved, and I carefully counted out the dollar bills and coins. I had just enough!

Rushing home but careful not to exceed the posted speed limit, I tenderly laid the dress on grandma's lap. I was stopped cold in my tracks when grandma pointed out that the dress was much too short for me to wear anywhere! My crestfallen face had no effect on her as she chastised me for wanting to look like Jezebel and have all the boys chasing after me.

I plaintively showed her that the full skirt allowed the dress to cover my knees when sitting, but she argued that it was indecent and the dress was never to be worn in public.

Sadly, I hung my coveted dress on the outside of my closet door and dreamed of walking into a banquet hall on the arms of Jimmy Wise as my classmates cheered and whistled. I wore matching white heels that sparkled with crystal rhinestones. My long brown hair was pulled up high, leaving wisps of curls around my face. A delicate touch of my favorite Honeysuckle perfume and a bit of soft pink lipstick provided a perfect finishing touch.

It was a dream that would never come true, but at least I was able to dream a little now.

Today, many years after grandma's death, I paint my toenails a bright red and wear a dainty ankle bracelet just to remind myself that's there's a little Jezebel in all women and that's not bad!

The first grading period at Ozark Academy was a surprise to me. On April 23, 1967, I received the first formal grades of my education.

I made 3 A's, 2 B's and 1 C (PE). Sandra made 1 F, 3D's and 1 C (PE).

My little sister was not doing very well and was not a happy child. She was frustrated and irritated.

Not only did she have to contend with extremely strict church school standards, but she also needed glasses and couldn't see the notes on the blackboard.

The kids made fun of her impetuous behavior, her homemade, ill-fitting dresses and lacking social skills. The teachers were insensitive and intolerant of any infraction of the rules.

*"Sandra went to school this morning but she was mad and got sent back home,"* I wrote on May 8, 1967. It was grandpa's 71st birthday and he was home for a few weeks. Sandra had wanted to stay home and celebrate a rare pleasant day with him.

Grandma had knocked her to her knees with a cracking slap across her face before pulling her out to the car and driving her to school. My attempts to assure Sandra that everything would be all right and coaxing her to be less aggressive and defiant were useless.

Grandma warned us that if Sandra got kicked out of the elementary school, we would have to move to a different school where Sandra could be better controlled.

She had a place in mind but first there would be an unexpected change to all our summer plans.

*Our dad poses in a rare photo with Sandra and Linda*

# Chapter 19

## Gone Fishing

On July 4, 1967, exactly one year after our dad had paid us the surprise visit in Missouri, grandpa got a call from his family in Tampa that his youngest brother Manuel "Uncle Mike" had suddenly gone into cardiac arrest and died. (The social security website I used for birth and death dates is incorrect. It says he died August 1, 1967.)

Grandma wouldn't hear of paying for a plane ticket but insisted that I drive him to Tampa for the funeral. We didn't know it then, but grandpa would never return to live with us again.

Grandpa, Sandra and I left for Tampa, Florida at 9 a.m. on July 5. Grandma couldn't hide her anger as we said goodbye. She didn't want Sandra and me going to Tampa without her because we were going back to the city of our Brantley relatives and she didn't want the family secrets to be let out of the bag.

By now grandma was Acting Administrator at Bry-Fern Nursing Home near Ozark Academy making it was impossible for her to leave without notice this time.

Sandra and I could hardly contain our excitement because we knew our dad was living in Tampa and we were cautiously but quietly ecstatic for the unexpected opportunity to see him and all our cousins we had missed over the years.

We arrived at the Mascunana house two days later at 9:20 p.m. Grandpa's family were grief-stricken and in mourning. Uncle Mike's death was a devastating blow to the Mascunana family!

Grandpa needed time to pull his relatives together and was relieved when daddy offered to let us stay with him and his family.

For the next two weeks we had unlimited time with daddy, our stepmother, Phyllis, our half sisters Jody, and twins, Jeanell and Jeanea.

Daddy took us to the beach and on picnics every day. We were euphoric with joy, and the carefree days rushed by as we relaxed with family, played with our sisters and cousins and went sea fishing with our dad.

I got horribly sunburned and broke out with terrible fever blisters on my lips, but I had never felt such exhilaration in my entire life.

Sandra was thrilled to be with her dad and became a joy to be around. She had no need to be a spitfire and bitter at the world.

Old rules were pushed to the back of my mind as I got a new bathing suit, a cute short haircut and enjoyed eating daddy's home cooked meals including tasty steaks we had never been allowed to eat.

Daddy and I spoke of our mother once, but he quickly killed the subject by saying he thought she was in Russia. I had always figured if I could ask my dad about our mom, he would answer the many unanswered questions, but that was the only time we made mention of my mom.

Our side of the Brantley family originated when grandma married Cecil Brantley. They had three children. Those children are: Our dad Robert (Bob) Brantley, another son, Bill (Cecil) Brantley and a daughter, Tina (Christine) Brantley Kruse-Scalise.

Our dad married our mom, Dorothy, and they had Sandra and Linda.

Bill married Louise and they had a daughter named Cindy (our cousin).

Tina was married to Harvey Kruse and they had 11 kids, Betty, Sharon, Judy, Diana, Jimmy, Tommy, Donny, Wanda, Linda and the (twins) Gary and Terry.

These are the cousins we remember best because we always looked forward to playing with them and later visiting any time we could get to Tampa. Sadly, several have died tragically.

Later, Tina divorced Harvey and married John Scalise but they didn't have any children.

Cecil divorced grandma (Brantley, at that time) and she later married Jorge Mascunana. They had one son, George Mascunana.

When grandma and grandpa got us, George Jr. was about 16 years old and enrolled at an SDA boarding academy (Fletcher).

George Mascunana married Rose Marie and they had five children: Karen, Jeff, Kevin, Greg and baby George Thomas who died soon after birth on April 19, 1965. I know that because I dedicated an entire page of my five-year diary to "Little George Mascunana."

Sandra and I never met Cecil (grandma's first husband), or knew of his whereabouts.

That's about as much detail as this book will delve into about the Brantley family. We remember grandma's brothers and sisters and their kids and a host of other Brantley kinfolks, but my very faded memory about the Brantley and Padgett relatives will not do them justice.

Enjoying our unexpected reunion with our dad and his family when we were young teenagers was thrilling but short-lived. On July 16, grandpa called us back to the Mascunana home. He had heard from grandma and she was sending money for Sandra and me to come back to Arkansas on the bus.

Sandra and I were terrified that she might show up at grandpa's house any minute and whisk us away again. We didn't want grandma to know that we had been staying with our dad, but nothing ever escaped grandma's all-knowing eyes and ears, and she wasn't going to allow this to last much longer!

Three days later, on July 19, 1967 I wrote in big letters,

***"GRANDMA CAME!"***

The next day I wrote a brief entry that concluded the only time in my life I enjoyed pleasant times with my dad.

*"We left this morning by jet plane at 15 till 8:00."*

Had I known this would be the last holiday I would ever enjoy with my dad, I would have hugged him a little harder and hung on a little longer.

It was a tragic day many years later when our dad died after a long illness. Phyllis Brantley, our stepmother, turned her back on Sandra and me the moment our dad took his last breath. She did not let me know about his passing and did not mention either of us in his obituary.

Sandra lived only a few blocks from their apartment and had often brought them homemade food or had frequently taken Phyllis to the store. We had no inkling she harbored ill feelings toward us!

During my last visit to see him a few months before he died, she was pleasant and kind as she had always been. We drove across the Gandy Bridge to pick up a favorite fish delicacy she and my dad enjoyed.

He had lived long enough to see my two sons, Billy and Philip. He had lived long enough to know that I had found our mother. He always called me, "babe". I don't think he ever knew my birthday or called me by my given name. His funeral could have been a rare supportive Brantley gathering with a U.S. military funeral for my dad. Instead Phyllis held a funeral service we were not invited to.

We tried desperately to find out what Phyllis had done with his body, but she turned her loyalty to her own daughters and cut off any contact with Sandra and me. It was unfortunate and heartbreaking – especially for Sandra who had placed her trust and confidence in our stepmother.

Years later Sandra and I found his final resting place in the same cemetery with other Brantley relatives.

His headstone reads, "Gone Fishing."

# *Chapter 20*

## *Tennessee Outpost*

After our trip to Tampa, grandma seemed more determined that Sandra and I would not continue school at Gentry. She made inquiry to Laurelbrook School in Dayton, Tennessee for us to transfer there.

Laurelbrook is another SDA School, but not accredited by the state. It is a self-supporting boarding academy for grades 9-12. The school puts heavy emphasis on spiritual education and requires students to work part of each day in the various departments operated by the school to help defray educational expenses.

It also has very strict rules for behavior and rewards any infraction with heavy doses of "free" labor.

I sadly told my friends and classmates at Ozark Academy goodbye. It had been a golden year in my life, but now we traveled 700 miles south to an outpost deep in the heart of Tennessee. It was almost like going back in time!

The only good part was that grandma would not be following us right away. Sandra and I moved into the girls' dorm that housed about 20 high school age girls.

Located on top of Walden's Ridge about 15 miles from Dayton, the school is set in the cool woods of the lovely rolling Tennessee Hills.

A small paved road cut through the mountain laurels and redbud trails to the main administration building that also housed the cafeteria and some small faculty apartments. The two dormitories lay nestled on each side of the cafeteria building. We could walk through the forest and across a swinging bridge to the 40-bed nursing home and the small school chapel.

All the buildings and houses on campus, including the nursing home, were built by student labor. The roads were dug out with the school dozer and gardens planted by students and staff.

The school was run primarily back then by Bob and Ruth Zollinger who controlled everything from the length of our hair and dresses to how much free labor would be meted out for infractions.

They also conducted the morning and evening worships, Wednesday night prayer meetings, Friday night vespers and several Saturday (Sabbath) Services.

We attended daily prayer bands, missionary bands and singing bands – all praising God and reminding us of His imminent return for His chosen faithful!

We soon became acclimated to the early morning bells for work and school. The regulations such as dresses below the knee (at all times), no make-up, no radio or TV, no secular music, a strict vegetarian diet and frequent worship and prayers, had already been strictly enforced by grandma.

The only new one that would soon get both of us into trouble, was the complete abstinence from any association with the boys on campus!

From the first day of our arrival, we were assigned to work. My diary indicates that I babysat faculty children, washed and ironed their clothes, chopped firewood, and cleaned houses.

Soon I was working the, "early morning kitchen." That meant getting up at 4 a.m. to start the ovens, get bread rising and peel potatoes for breakfast and dinner.

Within a few weeks I noticed I was getting some attention from the guys in my class and was surprised to discover that it was a nice feeling. Wow! Bill Peed, Bryan Sterner and Larry Miller were as polite and friendly as guys could be under the restricted environment! I would get fairly serious with two of them and get 10 hours of free labor for talking too long with one of them.

Fred Cash was a kid in the 7th grade who decided I was nice enough to be his "little sister". He later introduced me to his older brother, Bill Cash.

I didn't know much about Bill while I was a student Laurelbrook. Bill had graduated Laurelbrook two years before, but came up from Collegedale on weekends to visit old classmates. I had no inkling that Bill and I would be married within a few years!

My capable, sympathetic roommate, Barbara Sinclair, was a local girl whose parents lived down the road. She consoled me when the staff strip-searched our rooms and she educated me about the etiquette of living in modern housing with a dorm full of lively teenagers who did everything they could to bend the rules.

No one in the dorm appreciated a hot bubble bath more than I did! Only someone who had learned to bathe in icy cold creek water and wash their hair with a bar of soap, could know the soothing beauty of warm sudsy soap and the lovely fragrance of a simple perfumed bath.

Sandra was quick to make friends and found bookwork easier here. She still walked a tightrope but seemed to be happier. I was relieved for that and able to concentrate on my studies. I often played the piano for the many spiritual services and worked what seemed to be an excessive amount of hours in the kitchens and nursing home.

On Sandra's 16th birthday I record, *"Sandra got re-baptized today! I got her several small presents and 16 red roses. I also made her a chocolate chip birthday cake which is what she wanted."*

Also in the summer of 1968 I'm still wondering if I will ever find our mother. I have frequent headaches, back pains and sometimes limp with pain in my hips. I'm working from 4 a.m. until after midnight and my diary notes indicate that I'm losing weight.

To supplement the school's large vegetable gardens, they also purchased apples, tomatoes and fruits from local farmers. Preparation on the fruits and vegetables kept the kitchens busy almost 24 hours a day.

Nine months- one school year - is all we had free of grandma's control.

On May 26, 1969, grandma moved to Laurelbrook to teach in the elementary school. She moved into an old two-bedroom trailer about a mile from the school.

A few days later, I heavy-heartedly carried my belongings from the spotless clean bustling dorm to the foul smelling trailer filled with half unpacked boxes and clutter. Fleas already abounded and the odor of rotten food and uncleanliness permeated the air.

The next few days I worked feverishly to clean up the trailer and pick up junk from the yard before rushing to the school kitchen to supervise supper preparations for the 40 elderly residents at the nursing home.

Moving back in with grandma was a challenge but did present some unexpected opportunities for Sandra. She started sneaking out at night. I don't believe I ever told on her. I was glad for some freedom in her lonely life. I worried about her but thought she should finally make some choices on her own.

I too had a 'boyfriend' named Bryan Sterner, a Laurelbrook student whom I was writing to. I can't remember why, but I think he had been sent to another school for a few months because he got into too much girl-trouble.

Grandma or Sandra would mail my letters for me. I would name stars after him and write his name on trees around the school. He was too fresh and risqué for my taste, but he was the first guy to promise me the sun, moon and stars.

After one year and three months of calling Bryan my boyfriend, I wrote him a breakup letter on Christmas Day of 1968. Even though I idolized him, I knew I didn't need the kind of sun, moon and stars that he promised.

1969 was my senior year at Laurelbrook and with it increasing concern about what I would do with my life after that.

A review of my diary for that year shows me confused because grandma wanted me to marry Larry Miller who by this time had decided to become a SDA minister. I wanted to continue my education and study to be a teacher or a nurse although I was not sure where or how I could afford college.

Most girls back then were expected to get married and have children right after high school unless they entered college where the selection of a future mate could be made at a more leisurely pace.

I considered applying at Fletcher, North Carolina for the three-year RN course but didn't get that far. We looked at Southern College and other local colleges, but I didn't feel smart enough or secure enough to open those huge doors.

By my senior year at Laurelbrook, I could supervise just about any job on campus. I worked in the school kitchen, the nursing home kitchen and patient care. Some days I was assigned to the school laundry or the dorm cleaning crew.

Occasionally, we went off-campus for evangelical programs where I was required to provide special music on my flute or, Sandra and I would sing a duet.

We sang religious songs such as, "Ivory Palaces" and "This Is My Father's World" even though Sandra still disliked those songs with a vengeance.

November 15, 1968 we went to Chattanooga where I performed, "The Green Cathedral" on my flute *without a mistake.*

In the middle of my senior year I was thrown into turmoil when Sandra was kicked out of Laurelbrook for not abiding by the rules. Grandma and Mrs. Zollinger took her 350 miles south to Chunky, Mississippi where she entered yet another SDA self-supporting school.

I was devastated! It seemed like the last straw for me and I worried myself sick for some word on how Sandra was doing.

A few weeks later I left Laurelbrook with grandma's car without asking permission. I was going to see Sandra and I didn't care how upset grandma got. Nor did I think about my health. Without stopping to eat or sleep, I drove straight through to the tiny outpost in Mississippi.

But Sandra is a survivor and was doing great without grandma's hovering eye. She had discovered an old playmate, Alice Moon, from Avon Park. They worked together in the cafeteria where the food was plentiful and kids would meet all hours of the night without anyone checking up on them.

I was relieved and glad for Sandra, but had exhausted the last of my strength needed for the long trip back to Laurelbrook.

When I returned to Dayton several days later, grandma was waiting with all the vengeance of a mean old woman. She was angry that I took the car. She was livid that I went to see Sandra and she stood ready with her heavy wooden paddle to rip me apart.

I don't care anymore. Slowly I leaned over the trunk of the car and vomited on her feet as she raised the stick to hit me.

# Chapter 21

## Good-bye First Diary

December 30, 1968
Dear Diary...

"*Much has happened - and ended - since I started this. You have seen me through most of my teen years. Much is yet to come, but I thank-you for staying with me and being my friend when life was hard.*"

It's now January of 1969 I am in the middle of my last year at Laurelbrook. Grandma encourages a relationship with Larry Miller, but I'm unwilling to break the rules to get to know him better. He's friendly and always leads out in prayer bands. We have a lot in common. Larry has found four baby mice from the field and we are taking turns feeding them every two hours. He has them one day and I take care of them the next day. Three day later they die on my watch. We are both sad.

The bathroom at grandma's trailer has no running water and the tub is full of junk, so I often stay with my good friend, Johnnie Jones, on campus and take a hot bath and wash my hair. Her mom is also a great cook!

Grandma often gets tired of waiting for me to get out of class or off work, so I have to walk the mile back and forth to the trailer. The walking isn't as bad as the temper and angry words when I get there because she had to wait!

I write the words to a poem in my diary that I'd like to use in my life.

Maybe it's a song.

*"Guide me to those who need my help.*
*Teach me to see their need.*
*That I may speak the word that cheers,*
*And do the kindly deed.*
*And if the work that is appointed*
*Is what the world counts small,*
*Make me contented in my lot*
*And faithful in it all."*

I've also listed in my diary, 16 attributes for, "God's Woman" taken from Eccl. 31: 11-30.  It is the kind of wife I hope to be someday.

1.  *She knows how to sew – and does.*
2.  *She is thrifty.*
3.  *She gets up first in the mornings.*
4.  *She knows how to grow a garden.*
5.  *She is not weak, but healthy and strong.*
6.  *She stays in good spirits (verse 18).*
7.  *She dresses for health and not for fashion.*
8.  *She dresses becomingly.*
9.  *She is a good influence for her husband.*
10.  *She is able to help support the family.*
11.  *She is wise (smart).*
12.  *She knows how to say it and when to say it.*
13.  *She always has a gentle tone.*
14.  *Her family is well taken care of.*
15.  *She doesn't mind working.*
16.  *Her husband and children respect and praise her.*

May of 1969 was a busy month for us five seniors who had to write and practice our graduation speeches. We were getting ready for the junior-senior campout and still taking final tests.  I had to get up at 4 a.m. every morning for kitchen duty and was still sewing my graduation dress.

Then to top it off, less than one month before graduation day, Larry and I were punished with 10 hours of free labor for talking too long in the dean's office!

I thought it was the most unfair, unjust and stupid action the Laurelbrook Administration had ever done!

Larry, though, was remorseful (for talking?) and stood up at prayer meeting and apologized in front of the entire school body.

I wrote in my diary, *"This is downright confusing and discouraging."*

But in the end, he painted the entire school kitchen and cafeteria, and I painted the outside of every window in the girls' dorm the last few days of being a student at Laurelbrook School.

June 1, 1969 Dear Diary…

*"Today was a bright sunny day for graduation at Laurelbrook. We cleaned the chapel until 9:30 a.m. then showed up for the program at 10:30.*

*We held our breath as Larry marched in first because during practice he hadn't kept time to the music once! Then came Bill, Suzanne, Mary and me."*

Later I returned to the trailer alone and slept. I didn't say goodbye to any of my classmates. I would miss them and couldn't accept that I might never see them again. It seemed I didn't have the strength it would take to say good-bye to so many.

The next day I said goodbye to grandpa at the airport as he headed back to Tampa. Then I went back to my top bunk in the hot trailer, brushed off the fleas and went back to sleep for almost a week.

# Chapter 22

## A Kindness Never Forgotten

The summer of 1969 is very lonely. Most of the summer I do not write in my diary. I'm too sad to want the friendship of even a diary. My 19th birthday is a blank page.

Sometime in September of 1969, someone has a kind thought that will change my life forever.

Over on campus at Laurelbrook there is frustration in the Robert Flood family. They are not happy at Laurelbrook with all its strict rules and dictatorship management. They have decided to return to their roots in Dayton, Ohio with their two daughters and little son.

Kathryn Flood is a registered nurse. Kathryn has worked with me at the nursing home and we have become friends. She knows my future looks bleak and wants to make a difference.

"How would you feel about inviting Linda Mascunana to go back with us and take the LPN Course?" Kathryn asks her family at the supper table.

The family is excited to have me along and they invite me to go back with them and take nursing in Dayton.

Sometime in October I arrive in Dayton, Ohio to live with the Flood family for a year. Kathryn and Bob and their children, Juanita, Regina and Warren seem to enjoy having me around. I ride to work with Bob at Kettering Hospital every day. He works in maintenance and I work in Central Supply.

On Christmas day of 1969, I'm thinking of my family and wondering about my future. Grandma is living alone in that filthy trailer at Laurelbrook. I shouldn't miss her, but I do. I shouldn't worry about her, but I do.  Someone tells me that she is sick so I call Mr. Olsen at Laurelbrook and ask him to check on her for me.

Grandpa is in Tampa and everyone seems so far away.  There will be no packages from him this year.  I worry about him holding his family together and working too hard.

Sandra is unsettled and I'm often not sure where she is!  She won't be with me for Christmas and I feel lost without her.

Will I be smart enough to pass this nursing course?  Will I have enough money?  Will this family let me live with them for an entire year?

What about this relationship I've started with Bill Cash?  Already the Floods are not crazy about him.  But, he has driven all the way from Tennessee to Ohio to spend Christmas with me and he's the only solid thing I have in my life right now even if I don't understand it at all!  I enjoy the attention and crave the affection!

*Linda Mascunana, LPN*
*1971*

# Chapter 23

## Destiny Unfolding

*A small blue diary reflects my year in LPN Training, my engagement year to Bill Cash and the experience living in Ohio with the Flood family. At first I thought this diary might be too boring or intimate, but I'm grateful for the gentle nudging of this particular diary to transport you with me through the most significant year of my life!*

On January 1, 1970, I should have been resting up for the most extremely busy and exciting year of my life. I had the house to myself while the Flood family was gone on a holiday trip. Bill was returning to college in Tennessee.

I watched the softly falling snow dust the front yard and thought about Bill driving south. He shouldn't have bad roads, but might get tired and sleepy on the 400-mile trip that usually took him about 6 hours to drive if the car didn't break down. We're not engaged and there was a little pressure from the Floods for him to announcement an engagement. Our visits were few and far between and his letters were dependent on Bill's school load and other activities at college.

Watching the neighbor kids trying out their new Christmas sleds on the frosted grass, I was reminded of the long curving hill in Missouri that was so perfect for a thrilling slide on the ice. I used to scream at the top of my lungs as I neared the end of the exhilarating ride.

The quiet little village of Spring Valley had only about 500 residents and you could walk to most any store in town. The house was unusually tranquil without the busy clamor of Juanita, Regina and Warren. The laundry done and the house spotlessly clean, I looked for a good book and curled up on the couch.

Adjusting to the unusual silence in the house and feeling a bit lonely for Sandra, I was startled by the sound of the town's emergency sirens blaring over and over again. Finally I called the operator on the telephone and was informed that it was a barn fire on the edge of town and they were calling in all the volunteer firemen.

All afternoon I waited for Bill's call to say he had arrived back at college, but I finally fell asleep at 11 p.m. I woke up around midnight realizing I had forgotten to make any New Year's Resolutions and had no one to kiss under the Mistletoe.

The Flood family had offered me the best bedroom in the nice tidy three bedroom home. Little Warren had moved into the family room and the two girls shared a bedroom across the hall from my room.

The kitchen was clean, organized and convenient for making delicious home cooked family meals. Mrs. Flood believed in providing a healthful diet and always kept a good supply of fresh fruit and vegetables on hand.

Gathering around the table for breakfast and evening meals was something I'd never done. With grandma, we usually fixed our plate from pots on the stove when we got real hungry and found a place to sit that had the least clutter to move.

Now I felt special every time I said, "Pass the bread" and got a nice platter of warm bug-free rolls. (I wonder if they noticed me checking.)

Listening to the chatter of pre-teen girls and the cute lisp of a little five-year old boy was educational and refreshing. I had never been around kids that age!

But what surprised me the most was how everybody got up and started cleaning the kitchen after each meal! The only time our kitchen dishes got done at our house was when Sandra and I tried to make the trailer more livable by putting all the dirty dishes and spoiled food in large plastic bags and taking them to the edge of the woods behind the trailer when grandma was away.

We did that knowing grandma would whip us half to death for throwing away anything.

So, I was especially grateful for the post meal cleaning of the kitchen until it was back to its sparkling shine and aseptic clean fragrance! The kids may have fussed a bit about whose turn it was to help clean the kitchen, but no one ever heard me complain. It was always a relief to know that the food was unspoiled and the dishes didn't have the brown hard shells of roach eggs hidden on the backside.

The family had a few good laughs at my naiveness. I must have used an entire bottle of "conditioner" on my hair trying to get it to lather up! My clothes had always been kept in a box and I didn't own a pair of long pants. I had never been to a movie, gone bowling or listened to music on the radio.

The basement was referred to as the "cellar" and at first I would not go down there to use the washer and dryer alone.

Every time I flushed the toilet, I expected the water to chase me down the hall.

Little did the family realize how different my world was now. So many choices and all of them pleasant!

My first day of LPN School was January 26, 1970.

*"School seems frightening and scary, but I think I'll catch on."* *I wrote.*

Already some changes had to be made. There were not enough vehicles to go around at the Floods when it was time for me to start school. Through Mr. Flood's work contacts at Kettering Hospital, it had been agreed that I would live with Dr. Meng and his family for a couple months while attending the school downtown.

*"Everyone is upset and I'm confused"*, *I write in my dairy.*

Dr. Meng and his family had an extra vehicle and lived closer to my school.

*"I'm moving in with them today. Mrs. Flood is sad because she says I'll never come back and I really don't want my world upset again, but it seems like the best situation for everyone."*

Starting the LPN course also meant I could say goodbye to my full-time work in the Central Supply Department at Kettering Hospital where I'd been scrubbing dirty bedpans since December. I would be transferring to work as a nurses aide in a few weeks!

The Meng home was so large it seemed like a city to me. It was filled with modern conveniences I'd never seen before and the food was almost 100 percent Chinese. They had a garage bigger than any house I'd ever lived in. The large sparkling pool reminded me of the lake where I had nearly drowned as a child.

I shared a large beautiful bedroom with Nina who was also a guest-student. Our room had a large walk-in shower and we even had a phone beside our beds.

Later when school and work would wear me down, Nina would faithfully wake me up and push me off to my appointments on time.

Sometimes the Flood family would urge me to come back to live with them and I did try to visit often and help out if they called. Bill's dad visited me several times. Bill visited when he could but that wasn't much.

February 10 was an epic school day at nursing school. We wore our student nursing uniforms for the first time! I wrote in my diary, *"I need to gain about 15 pounds to fill in my uniform!"* I never grew tired of slipping into the light blue dress with an overlay of spotless white apron starched and ironed to a crisp. In my student nurse uniform I felt like I had slipped forward into my destiny and would never have to look back.

Unexpectedly, my world was turned upside down on February 18. There was an urgent call for me to contact the emergency room at Kettering Hospital.

Mr. Flood had been in an accident at work!

Rushing to the ER, I found him in a lot of pain and Mrs. Flood worried and terribly upset. His leg needed surgery but his condition was not good enough for the procedure. The doctor said he would be hospitalized for some time.

A few days later I noted that February 20 was an awful day.

*"They took Mr. Flood's cast off but his leg was covered with blisters so they couldn't do the surgery."*

I didn't move back to the Flood's home, but I stayed there much of the time after work and school to watch the kids so Mrs. Flood could be with her husband.

*"I'm working nights at Kettering and attending class by day. Sometimes I stay at the Floods and other times the Mengs need me.*

*I'm studying for anatomy tests and sleeping only a couple hours at a time."*

**February 25, Dear Diary...**

*"Another hectic day. I didn't have to work last night but got up early so I could stop by and check on Mr. Flood at the hospital. We had a nutrition test at school. When I got to the hospital for my afternoon shift, Mrs. Flood had me paged to tell me she needed me at home to stay with the kids. I fixed tacos for supper and helped the girls wash their hair. I washed and ironed my uniforms and fixed my lunch for tomorrow."*

Back in Tennessee there was a lot of unexpected activity going on. Sandra was getting married! This was a shock! I'd met Robert Neufeld a couple times and knew that his father was one of the doctors at Wildwood, but didn't think Sandra liked him that much.

The wedding was planned for March 8, only a couple weeks away! Before then, I had to make my dress for the wedding! This was added to my already frantic schedule.

On February 26, Mr. Flood finally had surgery on his leg and was slowly improving at the hospital. I was bouncing back and forth between checking up on him when I was at the hospital to watching the kids so Mrs. Flood could be with him.

The day before I left for Sandra's wedding, I attended a school program to watch Warren in a play and hurried back to Flood's to pack and get my uniform ready for school when I returned from Tennessee. Everyone was worn out and a bit discouraged at times.

*"Mr. Flood is finally sleeping tonight so he must be getting better,"* I wrote on February 27.

The weekend of Sandra's wedding, my dress was finally finished and the last test at school completed. I hitched a ride to Tennessee with friends from Kettering who had friends at Collegedale and arrived in time for the wedding rehearsal.

Sandra and Robert were married on March 8, 1970. I was her maid-of-honor and the day seemed too perfect. I already knew that Sandra did not love Robert and he didn't pretend to be kind to her. When we visited them, he had gone to the bedroom and slammed the door so hard the walls shook.

*"Sandra has done what grandma tried to do for me. The marriage is 'arranged' with grandma picking someone she thinks will be good for Sandra because his dad is a doctor and they are SDA. It is a copout of a bad home situation for both of them. I feel so sorry for Sandra!"*

But, combined with that promise is another promise made on that day.

**March 8, 1970, Dear Diary...**

*"Sandy and Robert sealed their vows with a kiss today and I sealed my promise to Bill. He asked me to marry him today. Words cannot describe how I feel. At moments I'm scared, but most of the time I feel so happy I could burst. Not for a fraction of a moment have I been sorry. I only pray to God that I will be given and will be able to give all that he ever needs and wants in a woman."*

We set the date of our wedding for his spring break in March of the next year and I headed back to Ohio for ten more months of school.

Arriving back in Ohio, I'm now off limits to any future young prospects my friends may select for me to date and also dependent on everyone for transportation. Whoever needs me the most provides wheels. Dr. Meng picks me up from school after I've waited two hours, and Mrs. Flood picks me up from Dr. Meng's house in the evening so I can help her.

At school I'm learning how to take vital signs and blood pressures. We learn how to give enemas and practice changing sterile dressings.

My schoolwork is challenging. Every day there are tests in something. I study nutrition, growth and development and nursing fundamentals. I memorize hundreds of medicines and their uses and side effects. I love every minute of it!

I try to be helpful at the Flood home and the Meng home because I'm so appreciative of the opportunity to take the LPN Course!

One night I help out at Flood's and another night I baby-sit little Elaine Meng while her parents go out. Sometimes I clean up after a big party the Mengs put on, or I stay with Mr. Flood during some bad moments at the hospital.

Many days I work eight-hour shifts at the hospital before or after class, sometimes forgetting what shift I'm supposed to work from one day to the next.

Every Saturday we are busy at church. The Flood family and I lead out in the Missionary Volunteer programs and I enjoy playing the piano for many services.

The highlight of every day is checking the post office for a letter from Bill. He doesn't write more than about once a week and sometimes two! He's often stressed and discouraged with his senior year at college and worries for the future.

Sometimes I'm distressed when I get a letter from Bill when he is depressed and unsure of our commitment or is questioning if we can afford a wedding. His car is always breaking down and he still doesn't know if he will be drafted when he graduates. So far, his college student status has kept him out of the war!

On March 12, a week after Sandy's wedding, Mr. Flood finally came home from the hospital. He's bedridden and needs constant care but now has a houseful of family to share the work. Everyone is thankful that he's improving!

As I rush in and out of the house, I notice that tulip bulbs and crocuses are peeking through the snow.

Because it was important to grandpa's Spanish heritage, we know that Bill will have to ask his permission to marry me.

Near the end of March, I catch another ride to Collegedale and we drive to grandma's trailer. When we arrive, there's no one living at the trailer! Even the cat, Tiny Tears is gone. After checking with the neighbors and making some phone calls, we found grandma and grandpa living in another town!

The next day, Bill did ask grandpa the question and after grandpa said yes, he presented me with the official Seventh-day Adventist symbol of engagement – a nice watch.

Right after that trip, I received $250 from the Social Security and my use of it became a big deal and probably the first major disagreement between Bill and me. Bill is not pleased because I want to loan the money to Sandy and Robert who I think really need it. Grandma wants to "borrow" it. I should use the windfall to pay my health insurance and defray living expenses, but I eventually sent it to grandma. I don't explain why in my diary.

Also during the month of April when spring flowers were blooming and the snow had melted, Sandra and Robert paid me a surprise visit. Not knowing where I lived, they went to Kettering Hospital and called me to come and get them. Even though I was nauseated from the many vaccines I had been given because I had no immunization history, we had a blast catching up on news. I was delighted to spend some time with my precious sister.

May 4 was a special day at school when we finally got our **nursing caps**! Every day for several weeks we had been hoping they would surprise us with our coveted caps, but first we had to endure tests in every subject and practice everything we were learning!

We were elated at our school, but in other parts of the state there was despair and sadness as four students at Kent State were shot and killed during a demonstration against the US invasion of Cambodia.

As the grind of almost full-time work and challenging days of school continue, I'm pushed to my limit. I feel so exhausted I wonder how I will make it through the next day. Many times I walk the two miles from school to the hospital to work the 3-11 shift and then sleep on the hard couch in the nurses' lounge.

The nights I sleep in the nurses' lounge, the security guard is kind enough to knock on the lounge door at 6 a.m. to wake me up. When I spend the night at Mengs, Nina pushes me out of bed after I've turned off the alarm too many times.

When I sleep at the Flood's home, I hit the snooze button so many times that the entire family is awake before I am, although historically, I've always been awake before the alarm goes off!

I moved back to the Flood's on May 19. I'm starting my clinicals at Kettering Hospital and transportation won't be such a problem. The Meng family gathers around to say goodbye.

Dr. Meng teases me and says there won't be anyone to help with supper dishes, and Mrs. Meng says there will be a quiet moment right after supper every night because that's when I always asked to be excused from the table.

I'm looking forward to finally getting a real patient. My first patient as a student nurse is a 31-year-old man who has cancer of the liver. He's only been married for a year and a half and they are expecting their first baby. It's such a sad situation, but I learn a lot about being a professional but caring nurse.

At the Flood home, I'm busy mowing the lawn, cleaning the house, fixing supper and washing and ironing for the family. I take the girls shopping or skating on Saturday night if I'm not working at the hospital.

May 24, during a rare phone call with Bill, he scolds me for something (perhaps for working too hard) and I start to cry. He has also called to say he hasn't written this week so not to expect a letter. The car has broken down again and he doesn't know when he will be up to visit. I miss him terribly even if we fuss a little.

After the call, I write in my diary, *"I wish I'd been the one to forget to say I love you."*

By June it's always cool at the hospital even though it's humid and hot outside. I'm taking care of older patients with diabetes and strokes and giving medicines for the first time. I have two patients and wonder how I will ever handle more than that. They say a regular nurse will have 12-14 patients!

By the middle of June I'm still working nights at Kettering Hospital, eating a donut and hot chocolate for breakfast and getting to school by 8 a.m. I write, *"It's pure 100% torture trying to stay awake working at night. I'm so tired during the day I make stupid mistakes that bring my grades down.*

A list of homework looks like this:

1.  Two Care Plans
2.  One diet coordinator plan
3.  Five bibliography cards
4.  10-12 medication cards
5.  Three Pharmacology plans
6.  Two study guides
7.  Test on diabetes
8.  Test on cardiovascular

My patient this week is a grouchy old man who, when I tried to help him stand up yelled, "Get your hands off me!" When I had to give him a bed bath, I didn't say a word and neither did he the entire time.

July 7 was a BIG DAY for me at school. I gave my first shot! My patient was a 50-year-old male in for a possible heart attack.

At first the needle just bounced off the man's skin. I said to my instructor, "Miss Corley, you do it" but she didn't say a word and I tried again. This time it went in halfway and I just pushed the needle in the rest of the way. Happily my patient was thrilled when I told him he was my first, "shot victim."

*On July 14 it's only seven months and 29 days before my wedding day. "I'm so sleepy in school that I'm ashamed. Bill called tonight and that really cheered me up. He was in a good mood but he was trying to watch TV and talk to me at the same time."*

July 20, 1970 I picked out my wedding dress at Penney's and put it on layaway.

Letters from Bill are few and far between. Many times after I call him, I note, *"He's really down in the dumps"*. Grandma sends a ten-page letter filled with reasons why I shouldn't marry Bill. Floods advise against the relationship.

Sometimes I wonder if I have a home anymore. Grandma's letters show that she doesn't want me to marry Bill and therefore doesn't care what I do with my life. She says she's on her way to California to be with her son, Bill, and doesn't leave an address. Grandpa (in Tampa) doesn't know where she is either. Sandra and Robert are not getting along and I never know where they are. The Floods know that my time with them is temporary.

But I'm in surgery rotation now and every day is something new and wonderful to learn about. One day it's a simple nose surgery but the day next someone has a serious by-pass operation. We watch the surgeries and take care of the patients when they have returned to the regular floor.

Suddenly it's September and not a word in my diary about my birthday. We are rotating in pediatrics now and I enjoy taking care of the little children. One baby has a heart defect that is successfully repaired.

September 10, 1970 my diary page is dedicated to my school chum from Laurelbrook, Karen Carlson, who got married that day.

*"Good luck, kid. To Tabby from Duflop". (Our nicknames for each other.)*

September 14. After several days of not hearing from Bill, I called him at midnight when I got off work. I'm heartbroken when it seems all I have accomplished is to interrupt a ballgame he is watching on TV.

*"After I hung up I felt like the bottom had fallen out of my world. I was terribly tired and the last thing I wanted to do was to go down to that cold lounge and sleep on that hard couch."*

September 16. *"I had a little boy who's in for a cord lengthening and he has a colostomy. He sure knows how to get his way – even if he has to frustrate it out of you… I tried to call Bill tonight but the phone was out of order…I went down to the cold, cold lounge and I was so tired and discouraged, I cried myself to sleep. I hope Delmar Siebert (the security guard) remembers to bang on the door and wake me up in the morning."*

Fall in Ohio is a beautiful colorful month with the leaves starting to turn colors and a slight coolness feels good on the bright moonlit nights. We started the exciting labor and delivery rotation.

On October 12, I watched in wonder and awe at the first birthing event of my career. I wrote, *"Mother and son doing well."*

Soon we were working as student nurses in the nursery and having a great time! I gave a bath to the little baby and took him to his mother at feeding time. We always hoped that each mother-to-be in labor would progress along so we would be there to observe the birthing events, but most of the time the labors continued long after we left the floor.

One mother-to-be was only 20 years old and especially frightened of the process. Someone had told her that the nurses would be mean and that the spinal would hurt real badly. She ended up wanting the spinal and saying that she couldn't have had the baby without us nurses!

By now I have found a good friend in a classmate named Bonnie. She has an artificial leg from a farm accident when she was a child but is cheerful and always optimistic! Sometimes I stay at her place or we go shopping together.

**October 22, Dear Diary…**

*"Delmar banged on the lounge door at 5:30 a.m. I went back to sleep until 6. I was cold all night and they had a Code 99 (Cardiac Arrest), at 2:45 a.m. so I didn't get much sleep. Today we watched our first C-section and two other deliveries! Tonight I went to prayer meeting with Floods, but I sure was sleepy!"*

**October 28, Dear Diary...**

*"I took care of a new mother today. (Her husband is real handsome!) They had a boy, which is what they wanted. I worked a double shift again today. Mrs. Flood called and said she is sick and doesn't think Bill should come to visit this weekend, so I told him not to come."*

**October 30, Dear diary...**

*"Bill called tonight to tell me he'd busted the car. The wedding expenses are extremely high, and he is almost certain of the draft when he graduates. We talked for 40 minutes but I'm not sure how much it accomplished. At the moment I'm totally confused about us and everything."*

**November 2, Dear Diary...**

*"Life looks hopeless! I need someone to talk to but I just don't know who or where to turn. A girl needs to be able to talk to someone!"*

**November 9, Dear Diary...**

*"Today I paid my last payment of $50 on my wedding dress. Bill called and said it's going to cost $300 to fix the car and that I won't see him until Christmas. I'm really tired. People came and went through the lounge all night last night and they had a Code 99 in the PICU at 4:30 a.m."*

In November I wrote a note to The Daily News Newspaper in Xenia, Ohio in response to its request for residents to write about things they were thankful for. The news clip is pasted in my diary.

*"I think I've been blessed with a wonderful year. Friends invited me into their home so that I could take nurses training which is almost completed now.*

*I have a good part-time job, and the most wonderful boy in the world has asked me to marry him. Linda Mascunana, 310 Wake St., Spring Valley."*

What I don't mention is that my part-time job is the night shift at Kettering Hospital and I'm in classes and working as a student nurse all day. Or, that I sleep in the cold nurses' lounge at night several times a week.

**November 25, Dear Diary...**

*"I was really lonesome when class got out and everybody went home for Thanksgiving. I worked 4-South and had 12 female patients.*

*I was so tired I kept bumping into doors."*

December was serious business in school as we learned about isolation procedures and I took care of patients acutely ill with multiple sclerosis and cancer. Many nights I'm sleeping in the lounge after a double shift, but Delmar has never once forgotten to bang on the lounge door in time for me to shower and get ready for school.

### December 12, Dear Diary...

*"We all went to church as usual today. I played the piano for what seemed like three hours. Tonight we went Harvest Ingathering but we didn't get much. Bill called tonight. He is so low. I worry about him. Grandma wrote anther ten-page letter. Guess she was down too! I sent Bill $70 from my check for the wedding expenses."*

### December 21, Dear Diary...

*"Mrs. Whitford was the teacher today. She always talks her full seven hours even if she doesn't have anything to say. My three hours of sleep last night didn't help either, but I did stay awake."*

### December 23, Dear Diary...

*"Today seemed like a million years. One of our patients died today but that only took away two hours. The other 14 hours took forever. Bill's car blew the transmission but he's coming by bus in time for Christmas!"*

I was learning early in my career that nurses don't get many holidays off! On Christmas Eve, while Bill played games with the Flood children, I worked 2-West at the hospital.

On Christmas Day we got a white Christmas, opened our presents and listened to Christmas music. The Floods would be gone for New Years Day and Bill was leaving again, but for today I rejoiced in a rare day off with a loving family and friends.

### January 3, 1971, Dear Diary...

Just three months before our wedding and I'm having serious doubts. The words in my diary will be an echo throughout the next 20+ years.

*"I called Bill collect person-to-person tonight and he accepted the call. He wasn't supposed to accept the call. Our agreement was that he would call me back at regular rates. I woke him up and he really complained when I mentioned that I accepted a collect call from Sandra last night. I'm sorry I bothered to call him. I sure don't feel any better. He kept saying, 'but I still love you anyway' after every*

complaint. *I don't want him to just love me anyway when I displease him. I'd give anything for him to understand me the way I am. He asked me if I was going to always accept everybody's collect calls... He just accepted mine!"*

Unfortunately, my diary is empty after I graduated from the LPN School and returned to Tennessee to start a new life with Bill Cash.

The simple entry on March 9,1971 are the words, *"Wedding Day."*

March 9, 1971

Robert William Cash III

&

Linda Jean Mascunana

# Chapter 24

## One Fine Day

It's only been four years since I put the hoe in the shed for the last time on Carver Creek, and said farewell to my faithful horse, Princess.

In those few years, I have graduated high school, passed the GED test, taken a 12-month Licensed Practical Nursing Course and passed the state boards for my LPN license. Sandra is married. Grandma is still seeking a peace she will never find. She does not approve of Bill Cash and refuses to contribute to the expenses of the wedding, but she and grandpa are planning to attend my wedding.

One month after graduating from nursing school, it's my wedding day! From barefoot teenager to blushing bride, I glide down the isle in a flowing white wedding gown and shoes that sparkle with rhinestones as I'm married to a smart young college graduate in a candlelight ceremony in Graysville, Tennessee on March 9, 1971.

My faithful diaries are silent and do not reflect my emotions of the most significant day of my life! The memories of that day must be retrieved from the recesses of my mind as I move piles of old boxes bursting at the seams and soiled with the age of time. There's a box labeled, "Wedding Album" and inside are pictures of many Laurelbrook classmates and staff members who have been a part of my life for the last few years.

My classmates, Charlie Brown and his twin brother, Andy, hold the main doors closed as the organ music begins. Tanta Lena Pike, the graying German lady who kept the nursing home clean and spotless, smiles from the end of one pew. My nursing school chum, Bonnie, beams with happiness. Johnnie Jones looks beautiful in her long blue bridesmaids dress. Grandma and Grandpa pose for a rare photograph together, and Sandra is the best maid-of-honor a bride could wish for.

I remember one thought that I had on my wedding day. *"I don't care if I am this happy for only one day, it will be worth it!"*

My long-flowing pure white dress sparkled with sequins and my face looked serene and incredibly happy beneath a simple white veil. I carried a lovely bouquet of flowers and Bill looked all grown up in his tux.

The selection of my dress was my major input for the wedding. I had put it on layaway, paying a little bit each month from the savings collected by working nights at Kettering Hospital during the year I attended nursing school in Dayton.

Bill and his family organized most of the other wedding plans. I felt that the ceremony and simple reception complete with a beautiful wedding cake, was just right.

Elder Dickerson, who had anointed and prayed for me so many times in Missouri, performed the simple candlelight ceremony. His theme was the story of Ruth in the Bible who would not leave Naomi. "Where you lodge, I will lodge. Where you stay, I will stay," she had promised and so he admonished us.

The Flood family served punch and wedding cake at the small evening reception before we headed off on our honeymoon to Atlanta, Georgia to attend a Globe Trotters basketball game and tour historic places in the area. No one had decorated our car, so I make a small sign for the back window that said, "Just Married."

My heart sang as I thought about the new life and exciting opportunities ahead. Life seemed perfect and finally safe and secure. I felt confident that life would be free of grandma's control, and the constant pain of rejection would be replaced with Bill's devotion and love for me.

Years later I would discover that my feelings on that "One Fine Day" were somewhat like a cat scratching in a sand box and expecting no one will ever know what lies beneath the surface. Unknown to either of us, we had much more baggage in the car than the one small suitcase I had lovingly packed for our honeymoon.

But for today, my world was at peace and I wasn't worried about tomorrow!

We couldn't imagine in our wildest dreams the news we would receive within a month that would change our lives forever.

# Chapter 25

## *Hyperemesis Gravidarum*
## *Don't Abort My Baby!*

Before cell phones. Before answering machines and long before cars had GPS systems to show one driving directions, I would spend hours driving home from work having taken the wrong turn from my first nursing job in Fort Oglethorpe, Georgia to our small newlywed apartment in Collegedale, Tennessee.

It wasn't that I didn't know how to follow directions or learn my way to and from work, but my mind was blurry after two months of severe, constant nausea and vomiting of pregnancy!

I had to pull over to the side of the road every few minutes with intense waves of dizzying nausea and powerful racking episodes of retching. I usually had to wave away several Good Samaritans who would stop to see if I needed help.

Hardly so. I just needed to kneel down in the grass to be sick or sit by the side of the road with my head between my legs to keep from fainting.

During the day at work while making round with the doctors on the medical floor and stopping at every other bathroom to gag and be sick, the concerned doctors would ask a few questions and confidently write out a prescription for yet another antiemetic drug that they assured me would get rid of the perpetual, awful nausea.

I accepted shots that knocked me out for hours, pills that didn't stay down and suppositories that made me sleepy for days!

In desperation, we bought most every natural product suggested by well meaning friends and relatives. Every time someone else mentioned, "Morning sickness. Eat some crackers," I was tempted to scream at them, "It's not morning sickness," but I didn't have the energy! This was nothing compared to morning sickness. The thought of a cracker: The odor of any food at all: Fragrance of any type: Lights, noise or motions – all tied my stomach in knots and started the uncontrollable retching again.

It continued unabated day and night. I felt miserable, repulsive and vile. I looked ghastly and felt exhausted and depressed.

Everyone, including the doctors, said it would stop after a few weeks, but this did not show signs of slowing down!

Bill was confused and frustrated. He had heard this might be physiological, and this assumption prevailed since no one had found any cause or cure for what we discovered had a name! **Hyperemesis gravidarum.** Excessive nausea and vomiting of pregnancy that could last the entire nine months!

Today there is much more information about this recognized disorder of pregnancy. It affects over 60,000 pregnant women each year making them unable to care for themselves or family. It prevents adequate intake of food and fluids and can last the entire pregnancy as mine did.

It causes prolonged fatigue, dehydration and metabolic imbalances. It can cause severe depression, and relationships can be badly strained. Thousands of women (25 percent) choose abortion out of desperation to relieve the misery and stress they face.

There's a foundation called HER Foundation that is devoted exclusively to understanding hyperemesis and it offers a network of support for all aspects of this often-misunderstood problem of pregnancy.

Mothers-to-be with HG are unable to tolerate blinking or bright lights, the sight, thought or smell of food and even noise or movement.

Those who care for mothers-to-be with HG should understand that she will need to mourn the loss of a normal pregnancy and missing out on the "fun" of being pregnant. She will need help finding the path to healing emotionally. Because doctors are reluctant to offer a treatment, and the cause is virtually unknown, she may feel guilty and ashamed. Others often blame the mother for this extreme reaction. It is expected that she will have difficulty being assertive or thinking clearly due to metabolic imbalances. She may risk starvation, dehydration and need IV's for hydration or even a feeding tube for nutrition.

Mothers with HG often don't ask for help when they need it. They should be surrounded by loving people who understand them and will be supportive in times of depression and with their feelings of helplessness and dependency. There is the longing to eat and drink normally, the feeling of isolation and the inability to prepare for the arrival of the baby.

Perhaps the most frustrating for those who suffer with HG, is other people's perception that all this is only in her mind! I know all this to be true because I can remember feeling this way so many times and knowing that no one understood what was happening to my body. I did feel responsible, not only for the unplanned pregnancy, but I constantly searched my mind for something terrible I had done to cause such catastrophic sickness.

But we had even more trouble on the horizon. Bill had just graduated from college with no job promise because Uncle Sam was beckoning to the call of war. Now it looked like I couldn't hold down a job much longer if this excessive sickness didn't stop. Bill simply didn't know what to do with me.

Finally, it was decided that we would move in with his parents in Maryland where he could work with his brother roofing houses, and I could try to work part time. I would be welcome to stay there until I was on my feet again if he was sent overseas.

The packing and travel made me feel even worse. Movements, riding in a car and bright lights were all the things I shouldn't have been exposed to, but we didn't know that and I didn't have a choice. With no privacy for the constant retching that was aggravated by the movement of the car, I was almost out of my mind by the time we arrived and, I was extremely ill!

Bill's parents quickly helped him find medical care and a reputable doctor. I remember sitting with Bill looking across the doctor's massive desk and listening to his discouraging options. I felt like I was an object being spoken about and not addressed as a person. He said the only thing that would stop the nausea was an abortion.

Directing his words to Bill, he said he would be willing to terminate the pregnancy if that was what I wanted.

I realized that if I didn't take a stand for my baby, or if I got so sick that I couldn't make a decision, that might be the end of my pregnancy! We both wanted our baby more than anything! It might not have been planned, but there was never a question about how delighted we were to know we were going to be parents!

Right then and there, I made Bill promise in front of that doctor that no matter how sick I got, or even if I ASKED for an abortion, that he would PROMISE me that it would NOT BE DONE!

It was agreed that an abortion would not be a solution, and I knew that I wouldn't take any more medication for the nausea. That was about three months into a very long nine months.

The doctor said one good thing in my favor was that each time I was sick, I would have a few minutes of peace before the nausea started again. He urged to me eat as often as I could even if it didn't stay down very long. I would get some nourishment from the food, he said.

Back then good Seventh-day Adventists did not drink carbonated beverages that had caffeine added, but when a well-meaning friend suggested that Coca-Cola might help relieve the nausea, I tried it and found that at least it didn't burn my throat coming back up like 7-Up did! I was embarrassed to have the family watch me sipping ice cold Coke, but in the end, that was the only fluid that I could tolerate.

So, my first real experience with Bill's parents was not under the best of circumstances. I don't think I ever got to put my best foot forward during our entire 20-year marriage. I always felt that I walked a tight rope and that my many talents were rather trite by their standards. They were always kind and loving, but I often had the feeling that I didn't quite measure up. Major decisions were made without my input and our personal problems came under parental scrutiny. The first year of our marriage set the stage for the emotional roller coaster that never quite got a chance to slow down.

During that long hot summer of 1971, Bill worked from sunrise to sunset on the hot roofs with his brother, Lerry. They made a good team and both worked hard. Sunburns turned to suntans and the days melted together with no letup in my sickness and no information on what the future held for us.

By summer's end, I knew we couldn't continue living with his parents.  I didn't want to be a burden especially if Bill wasn't gong to be there.  One day someone came up with an unusual but excellent idea!  Why not go back to Laurelbrook School at Dayton, Tennessee .  Bill could teach until he was called up and I could work at the nursing home when I felt better.  The calls of inquiry were made and we were accepted!

So off we went again, pulling our little U-Haul trailer behind us and holding the little pink bucket between us!  Now I was six months pregnant.  We had been married seven months.  We had moved twice, and I was looking to get my nursing license in the third state before I'd worked one year.  It's a good thing we were needed at Laurelbrook because by now neither of us were good placement material!

We set up housekeeping in a small trailer on the back property at Laurelbrook.  Water and sewer was sporadic and we were fairly isolated back in the wooded area, but I deeply appreciated the solitude and finally knowing that we would have the stability of our own home and work for both of us.  We wouldn't have any money because Laurelbrook paid "in kind" and we were obliged to follow the strict regulations of the Seventh-day Adventist community, but medical expenses would be covered and food was always available.

We were both returning to familiar people and friends.  Bill quickly became entrenched with teaching and the responsibilities of being a staff member.  I was allowed to work short hours at the nursing home in the afternoons when the nausea was slightly less intense by my eighth month of pregnancy.  I trusted my doctor down in Dayton who said the baby was doing well.  I felt well enough to play my flute with the student choir for the Christmas programs! And, it looked like Bill might not be drafted after all!

# Chapter 26

## The Day Before Billy Was Born

"*I* hope I sleep good tonight and that tomorrow is better than today," I wrote in my diary on the evening of January 6, 1972. A few hours later the birth pains of our first child wakened me.

It was midnight and even though my water had broken and I was having labor pains every three to four minutes, I refused to leave for the hospital. I told Bill that first-time mothers took "hours and hours" and I didn't want to get there and be sent back home because I wasn't far enough along yet!

But it only took another half hour for us to realize that this was for real! The pains were strong at every two minutes! We arrived at Rhea County Hospital in Dayton at 1:15 a.m. The nurses said I was pretty far along and started getting me ready for the delivery room immediately. The fetal heart tones were steady at 128 and the baby showed no signs of distress.

At 2:30 a.m. they allowed Bill into the "labor room" where I had been given a shot for pain and a mask to breathe into when the pain was real bad. Within 15 minutes I was ready for the delivery room and put to sleep. At 3:05 a.m. Billy was born. He weighed 7 pounds, 8 ounces and was 20 inches long. At 3:10 a.m. Billy went to the nursery. At 3:25, I was back in my room and at 3:45 a.m. they brought our firstborn son into the room. We named him after his dad, Robert William Cash the 4th.

Billy was born ten months after our wedding day, less two days. While not the plan we had agreed on, it was the first of many unexpected changes that would happen during the first year of our marriage. During that time, Bill had finished college. I had graduated from nursing school. We had moved twice and Bill narrowly avoided the draft (by one number!) during wartime.

My experience in the hospital after Billy's birth was amazing in many ways. It was the first time I could remember not being sick to my stomach. I had lived with nausea so long that I had honestly forgotten what it was like to feel hungry! And those pain pills they gave me! I had no idea how one little pill could put one into such a euphoric state of well-being.

My body was so worn out and run down that I slept the entire day except when they woke me up to hold Billy every three hours. Dr. Littell said I had to stay an extra day at the hospital. My roommate came and went. Bill wasn't allowed to visit when I was sleeping.

My doctor was familiar with the day-to-day life at Laurelbrook. He said it was like his second home because he treated every staff member on the campus and was the medical director for the nursing home. He knew that everyone worked hard and rarely had any time off to rest and relax.

By the time Billy was born, Bill knew he had missed the draft and could put himself wholeheartedly into his commitment to Laurelbrook. For now, he enjoyed teaching and supervising the students at work.

## Baby Talk

Billy and I arrived home when he was four days old.

*"He is the sweetest little angel ever born,"* I wrote in my diary that night.

The next morning I was still weak and very shaky, but gave him his first official bath with Grammie Cash looking on. *"He didn't cry at all."*

When Billy was seven days old, he slept from 5 a.m. until 10 a.m. – the longest time yet! I was still very weak and not able to be up much. Mom Cash helped me wash my hair.

*"I sat on the couch for the first time today,"* I wrote when Billy was seven days old.

January 18. *"Billy's first doctor's visit. He weighs 8 pounds and I weigh 105 pounds!"*

*January 28. "I'm getting sleepier and sleepier and Billy is sleeping less and less. Billy has a little cold."*

When Billy is one month old, we notice his first smile and he gives everyone a look that says, "Where did you come from?" Today he fell asleep when we were taking pictures of him! Billy weighs 9 ¼ pounds and is 22 inches long!

February 16 at 3:15 in the morning, Sandra calls to say she has gone into labor and is going to the hospital. Billy's cousin, "Bobby" Neufeld is born at 5:51 a.m.

A few days later, Billy and I spent four days with Sandra, Baby Bobby and his dad. When Billy and Bobby took turns crying during the night, Sandra and I had to figure out which baby needed to be fed! We had a good time those few days! Even though we were tired and sore, we took the babies to K-Mart and over to Wildwood Sanitarium and School to visit relatives.

Times would get unspeakably difficult for Sandra within a few months, but for now we were blissfully unaware of the severe challenges closing in on her and Bobby.

Billy takes his first antibiotic for a bad cough when he's not quite two months old. Bill and I can't agree on where Billy should sleep. I want him with us when he's sick but Bill thinks he should stay in his crib. (I win!)

At three months, Billy is smiling a lot and likes to play with his rattle! Mr. Marlow is complaining because I'm not back working at the nursing home yet! I had been allowed six-week leave when Billy was born, but so far found that it was impossible for me to pull myself away from my firstborn and leave him in the care of immature teenage students.

Refusing to leave Billy, I demanded more time at home. Bill argued that everyone on campus had to work their fair share, but the coaxing didn't budge me and Laurelbrook had to find work I could do at home.

April 25 was a monumental day because Billy turned over for the first time! I left him on his stomach for his nap and when I returned, he was on his back.

Bill and I have been married for a little over one year and already I'm feeling alienated from my husband. I write in my dairy that he reads at the table while I want to chat and spend time with him, and he stays up to read many hours after I beg him to come to bed.

*"He says I'm clingy,"* I complain to my diary.

But Billy is our joy and sunshine. On May 16 when Billy is four months old, I record that he is cute and happy. *"He really laughs when you tickle him,"* I write.

In June, when Billy was almost six months old, we moved from the trailer into the girls' dorm where I was to be the girls' dean. Bill had been hoping to be selected as the boys' dean and I don't know why he didn't get that appointment, but here we are in the girls' dorm.

Bill was delighted to have a closet of his own. Billy had a small bedroom that is "little boy decorated" but used mostly for taking naps! As Bill predicted, Billy has learned that if he cries, I'll bring him to our bed.

On July 1, Billy is pulling himself forward with his hands and that is so cute. Everyone who sees this unusual style of crawling gets a chuckle! He loves for Bill to run with him in the stroller and can sit up straight in the stroller for a few seconds. He is eating "quite a lot" of baby food and holds his bottle.

Bill spends time up at the trailer where we used to live listening to music with students. He works late every night in the darkroom on the yearbook or on some activity with students. I write that he seems in a daze. *"I hope he's not upset about our move to the girls' dorm."*

In August, Billy gets around by "creeping" and has learned to crawl up the four steps from the living room to the kitchen.

By my birthday in September, Billy is starting to get up on his feet by holding on to a table or chair. Once he pulled himself up by holding on to my skirt! He is starting to say "ma-ma" and "dab, dab, dab" and "ba-ba". (Is that Spanish or English?)

On September 10, (eight months almost to the day), he cut his first tooth "lower front left". Please note that this tooth was not there when I checked in the morning, but I felt it with my fingers in the afternoon!

November 1, Billy has four teeth and has been "crawling real well" on his hands and knees for about a week. He can also find his bottle and feed himself at night and refuses to be rocked to sleep.

On December 11, at eleven months of age, Billy took his first steps!

By Christmas Day, Billy has seven little teeth and is starting to pick up and eat table food. He enjoyed lots of presents, some from the students who loved having a baby around the dorm.

Billy always enjoyed outings with me to the little town of Dayton where we would always find some little toy or meet Grandma Mascunana (and sometimes Grandpa Mascunana) for some shopping or a little meal together. His baby talk was so original that I wrote it down just like it sounded. Once during a trip to town, Billy and I had this conversation.

"Grandma has gone to Florida to see Grandpa."

"Etts go to forida in good morning to see gamma."

"Oh, you'll have to ask your daddy a big request like that."

"Daddy 'ill say no."

"And what happens then?"

After a deep sigh, Billy says, "Daddy 'ill say no and I 'gess ee 'ont go."

# Chapter 27

## *May I Take a Message?*

It wasn't long before Bill was appointed Dean of Boys and we moved from the girls' dorm into a small two-bedroom apartment at the boys' dorm. I worked part-time as a nurse in the nursing home and was dorm-mother to 30 boys.

A typical day would began something like this:

Ring…Ring…Ring

Is anyone going to get that phone? Where's Bill? Does anyone care that I worked the midnight shift?

After stumbling into the living room to answer the phone, the conversation would go something like this.

"Where's Bill!"

"He's not here."

"When will he be back?"

"Probably not before midnight."

"Well, when you see him tell him to make the boys quit peeing out the back second story windows!"

That message was from the president of the school, Mr. Bob. Most messages for Bill were complaints about something and Bill didn't handle complaints very well. Bill's agenda for each day was usually a three-page list in his small intricate handwriting. If he couldn't follow his list, he was usually in a very bad mood for all of us.

My days were always hodge-podge, never ending and never the same.

Now with baby Billy, I was even busier and my time was still in demand from everyone.

Our dorm rule for the dean's apartment was to knock and enter. The guys would stand in the doorway and yell for Bill or me. From the bedroom, I would whisper-yell that I was with the baby and Bill was not home, but since the boys couldn't hear me, they would wander around looking for one of us until they got to the bedroom. Then they would carry on the conversation with relief at having found someone to help with their problem.

Occasionally I would walk into the woods to rest and play quiet tunes on flute. Wildflowers were in abundance and small wild animals would soon be scampering around me.

Nearby was the school chapel where I would slip in to play the piano or organ. The music would resound across the school campus and before long someone would peek in and start a conversation that would end my solitude.

One morning I didn't get up to answer the phone. It had been a long night up with Billy and I didn't think I could handle another give-Bill-this-message call. But when I didn't answer the phone, people were soon banging on the door, tapping on the windows, and the phone didn't stop ringing.

Who was going to check on the sick boys and give them a written release from class and work? Where was the boiler boy? The dorms were cold? Why didn't John show up for his free labor in the kitchen this morning? Could Joe have cough medicine? Did Jeff have appendicitis? Would Bill teach an extra class this morning because another teacher was out sick? Would I conduct worship tonight so Bill could attend another meeting?

"No, John you don't have a fever. Yes, Tom I have diarrhea medicine for you. How many times did you throw up last night? When did the pain in your side start? How long have you had this earache? No, you can't get up for recreation tonight."

Each morning I would inspect the dorm rooms and give notes saying they could have lunch because their room was clean. I would answer the constantly ringing phone and take never-ending messages for never-available Bill. Boys would be in and out of the apartment day and night, talking, complaining, asking, or just sitting around watching me work.

In the afternoons I worked at the nursing home, usually from 2 – 6 p.m. There I would supervise students as they learned how to care for the elderly as nurse's aides, in housekeeping or in the kitchen and laundry. In addition I gave medicines, did treatments, noted doctor's orders and kept a nursing eye on the condition of the 40+ patients.

Living in the boys' dorm was like swimming in a fish tank. The boys assumed I was home-away-from-home mother. Could they use my washer? Could they bake a cake in my kitchen? Would I take them to the store? Could I sew this shirt or fix these pants?

I listened when they were fed up with all the rules. I advised when they thought they were in love. I consoled when they got bad news from home or were homesick. I intervened when they got mad at Bill. I intervened when he was mad at them!

In return they fixed the dryer when it broke, repaired the commode when it leaked and sometimes they rocked the baby to sleep.

One day when Billy was almost two years old, someone had started to bake a cake and left the burner on. I entered the kitchen to find the kitchen on fire with flames leaping to the ceiling.

Strangely, there wasn't a boy in sight!

Little Billy exclaimed at the fire burning brightly, "Look, look, big light!"

I yelled for help as I grabbed Billy and ran out of the apartment. By then several boys were on it. Lee grabbed the burning pan and ran backwards out the door with it. Another boy dumped my canister of sugar on the fire and someone else turned the water hose on it.

Later, the president of the school called for Bill. Seems the boys had a snowball fight with the girls and he wanted everyone punished. The president's wife came over to see me and said I did too much for the boys. She fussed at me because I let them bake the cake. She said I should spend more time keeping the apartment in order and that Bill shouldn't work so hard. She said those boys didn't deserve so much and I would spoil them.

She complained about my absence from staff worship services. She didn't want me sharing the washing machine with the boys because the school would have to pay for any replacements. We should eat in the school cafeteria more often. We needed to keep the dorm quieter. Rarely, if ever, was there any thanks for our work.

But we stayed while Bill got more frustrated and unhappy with the system.

When Billy was a little over three years old he got his baby front teeth capped because they were brittle from too many night bottles. May 24, 1975, was a very bad day for Billy and me. I wasn't allowed to be with him, but sitting in the front office I could hear him whinefully fussing and saying, "uch-ohhh" as the dentist worked on his teeth.

He came out of the dentist's room looking quite distressed and fussing a little. As I got him a cool drink of water, he said to me, "Mommy, I didn't die!"

"Did you think you were going to die?"

He nodded and said quietly, "yes. I 'most died."

# Chapter 28

## *Oh How He Howled!*

In August of 1974 when Billy was well past two years old, the older women on campus were tisking me for not having Billy potty trained.

Yes, he could follow simple instructions. He was able to stay dry for more than two hours at a time. But he wanted nothing to do with the little blue potty chair in the bathroom. I tried all the things it suggested in my baby books like letting him run around naked and some things not in the book like giving him candy when he agreed to sit on the potty chair!

Finally I decided to skip the potty chair and assume if he wore training pants, he would be more cooperative. Boy, was I in for a surprise.

The diary entry for August 27 reads, *"I put training pants on Billy tonight. Oh how he howled, screamed and got quite hysterical!"*

But, within three days Billy had figured out the purpose of pants and that he could easily pull them up and down. His potty-training days were almost over!

It was a good thing too because by now I was about six weeks pregnant with another baby, and while the nausea wasn't as bad this time, August was the most miserable month.

Perhaps this time I would be blessed with the usual morning sickness and could enjoy a rather normal pregnancy!

Six weeks earlier Bill has rushed me to the hospital in the middle of the night with sharp piercing pains in my abdomen. Within the hour, I was in surgery for an emergency exploratory to rule out an ectopic pregnancy.

"She can't be pregnant. She failed the pregnancy test," Bill said

I remembered all the times in Missouri when grandma had put a washcloth soaked in lemon juice on my aching left side and by morning the pain would be gone. No one was interested in trying that cure this time.

The moment I woke up from surgery, there was no question in my mind of the diagnosis! I was experiencing the familiar sickening nausea. Not just sick to my stomach, but nausea in every cell of my body!

Two days later I went home to recuperate and perhaps the surgery was a blessing because now I had to lie still and do nothing. I wasn't allowed to lift Billy or do heavy work.

I could lie out in the sun and feel the peaceful sunrays on my face and let the natural forces of nature heal my body – both inside and out. Most of all, I didn't need to feel guilty about relaxing. That burden was taken from me and for the first time in my life, I could focus on myself and take care of me instead of everything and everyone else!

Yes, I was wretchedly sick. On July 19, the only words in my diary are: "Try throwing up with a bunch of stitches in your stomach."

We cancelled a planned vacation to Florida. (Our first!) We decided instead to take a short trip to the Smoky Mountains near Knoxville.

On July 24, we took a long day-trip to Clingman's Dome, the highest mountain in the Great Smoky Mountains National Park.

Driving along the ridge of the Smokies can be spectacular if one is not already seasick. I don't know if Billy remembers the three bears we saw, but I still recall the dizzying heights and the congested winding roads that went up and down, around and around.

By my birthday on September 3, I was feeling better if I remembered to take the medication, Bendectin, at night. If not, I felt extremely nauseated most of the morning but able to take care of the family in the evenings.

Our friends, Neil Hunt and Floyd Phillips were around a lot helping out with Billy when the nausea got the best of me. They tackled household repairs that Bill couldn't get to. I was able to work at the nursing home most afternoons so I pulled my fair share there. The rest of the time, being a dorm mother kept me busy and on my toes!

Billy was sharp and noticed more than I realized. One morning a student came into our apartment complaining of feeling sick to his stomach. This was nine days before I gave birth to Philip. I still had some nausea off and on but it was mostly in the mornings and mild. After I'd given Walter some medicine to settle his stomach and sent him back to his dorm room, Billy asked, "Mommy, is Walter going to have a baby too?"

A few days later, on the evening of February 18, 1975 at about 10:15 p.m. when I was running bath water for Billy, I started into labor. We didn't know if would be a boy or a girl but we told Billy the baby was coming and we had to leave (quickly) for the hospital. Billy got quite frightened and begged to go with us. He pleaded to go along and offered to wait in the car. It was very cold outside, but we asked our babysitter, Joe Stevenson, to come along and we piled into Neil Hunt's car for the 12-mile trip to the hospital.

By 10:30 p.m., we were at the hospital and I was being admitted because the baby was indeed well on his way into the world.

At midnight I was walking in the halls with a few pains that I could handle, but the nurses told me that it wouldn't be long. At 1:45 a.m. the pains were quite strong, and I was given a shot to take the edge off. By 3:30 a.m., I was in the final stages of labor and on my way to the delivery room.

As he had promised, Billy was content to wait in the car looking at books. Back then hospitals didn't allow kids in the waiting rooms. But, about 3:30 a.m. Joe got chilly and took Billy to the front lobby to wait.

Philip was born at 3:37 a.m. on February 19, 1975. Baby Philip weighed 6 pounds, 8½ ounces. He was 20 inches long. Later I wrote, *"He was alert and had no hesitation or trouble crying."*

Soon Dr. Littell came through the lobby having already delivered baby Philip. He told Billy that he had a baby brother. Billy stood there just blinking up at him until he left. At that point, Billy turned to Joe and said, "You mean it came out?"

A few minutes later Billy was allowed into my room to see the baby. That was a very rare privilege indeed!

I was in labor for extremely short periods of time with each child. Most mothers back then experienced the birthing pains for at least 12 hours and sometimes 48 hours. Billy and Philip blessed me with less than 3 hours of labor and only an hour or so of hard childbirth pains.

Sadly, I was put into a "twilight sleep" for the actual births of Billy and Philip and didn't hear the first cry of either one. Today, most mothers are given an epidural and feel no pain but are awake and alert for the birth. Twilight sleep was found to cause an increase in post- partum depression and is not used much these days.

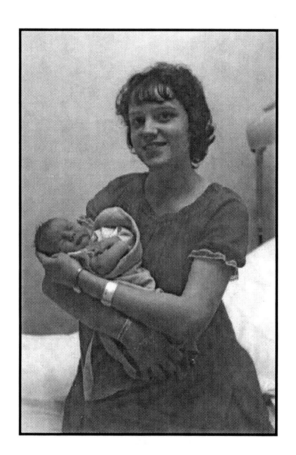

**Baby Philip & Linda**
**2-19-1975**

# Chapter 29

## Happy Mother's Day, Mommy

On Mother's Day, May 11, 1975, I hugged my two little sons and thanked God for blessing me with such perfect beautiful children. I wondered if I would ever find my own mother and wish her a Happy Mother's Day.

Philip came along three years after Billy. He was tiny, quiet and almost no care at all. Feed him, hold him and rock him back to sleep. I thought he would be my baby forever. He did not become a mama's baby but he is a loving son who is a tall good-looking, talented educator. He loves his independence and uses his creative freethinking mind to help his students succeed in life.

When Philip was a baby, I wrote a "six-month report" that goes like this.

*"Philip weighs 16 pounds and wears size 9 month clothes. He has no teeth but chews on his fists when he doesn't have a pacifier.*

*He wakes up at 8 a.m.and does best if given a bottle (usually propped up in hopes he might go back to sleep) or I get him up for a bath and to get dressed. He plays with his fists a lot and says "ahhhhh" loudly to Billy and himself.*

*About 10 a.m.he is fussy and I feed him a jar of baby food adding cereal and formula – Similac with Iron - and he either goes to sleep while being held with a bottle or halfway cries himself to sleep.*

*Just about the time I'm sitting down for lunch, he wakes up and is usually put on a blanket outside and entertained by boys until 1:30. I give him another jar of baby food and a bottle of formula before his afternoon nap.*

*He's a little fussy in the evening unless I can be outside with him. About 9:30 p.m. he gets a jar of junior food and goes to sleep in my arms with a bottle.*

*Sometimes Billy and Philip wake each other up. It's best to put both to bed at the same time with Billy looking at books. It's funny when they talk themselves to sleep."*

Philip turned over for the first time when he was a little over four months old. On June 27, 1975, I wrote, *"He pushes himself backward on his back with his feet. He holds his chest up when on his stomach and stands stiff when we hold him by his fingers. He laughs at anyone who talks to him and is just starting to hang on to me when I carry him in my arms."*

At 9 and ½ months, Philip started crawling well (the last week of October). He now weighs 20 pounds and is putting everything into his mouth although he has no teeth yet. He enjoys pulling himself to a standing position but loves to rock back and forth on his knees. He likes a pile of toys to plunder through. He laughs all the time.

On January 12, 1976 at almost 11 months, just before his first birthday, Philip took his first ½ step all by himself. Billy has just turned four years old.

As I was reviewing my dairies for this book I came across a childish note on January 7, 1978 that says, "Today, I'm 4 years old. Billy. Now who put that there?

It also says, *"Yes, and what a big day! Your presents were on your toy chest when you woke up. I called you from the San and sang happy birthday to you. Kids came at noon for cake and ice-cream and we had a birthday supper".*

For several days before his birthday, Billy had told everyone about it. He was excited about turning four years old and looked forward to a birthday party.

I enjoy the little chuckles I get from reading the tid-bits about my boys when they were little. About the time Philip was taking his first steps, Philip woke Billy up in the night by saying very loudly, Dada- Da-Da-Da.

Billy says to Philip, "Daddy's 'teeping, Philip!"

Philip carries on just as loud and demanding.

"But Philip, daddy's teeping in bed. Dis is big buder. Don't you know?"

My diary records that Billy was becoming a math wiz at four years old too.

*"Billy can count to 6 sometimes,"* I wrote.

On March 3, 1976 Billy went with his dad to math class. For fun, Bill asked Billy some questions in front of the students.

"Billy, how many is 1 + 1?"

"Two"

"How many is 1 + 2?"

"Tee"

"How many is 2 + 1?"

"Tee"

"How many is 2 + 2?"

"Tor"

"How many is 1 + 3?"

"Ahhh, tor"

"How many is 2 + 3?"

"Two and two and one or two and one and one and one."

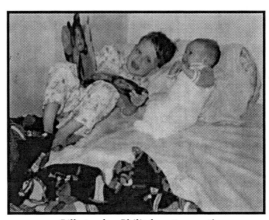

*Billy teaches Philip how to count!*

# Chapter 30

## *We Forgot About the Glue*

"Mommy, when daddy goes to Europe, I can go with him and one of my Teddy Bears can be daddy."

Billy wanted to be a world traveler from an early age!

Four months after Philip was born, Bill was preparing to go to Europe with his parents for the church's General Conference. We had debated if I should go with him. Thinking that the new baby would be too young for such an extended trip and not wanting to leave either of the boys behind, it was decided that I would not go. I wonder if this decision set the stage for future events, vacations and trips when I usually stayed at home to work.

Even when the boys got older and went on excursions with their dad, we didn't make "togetherness family time" starting with when the boys were small to when they were teenagers.

They enjoyed ski trips, camping trips, Pathfinder Camporees, baseball games, and other sporting excursions with their dad while I stayed at home to keep working. Later, when Bill took trips overseas, I didn't accompany him on those once-in-a-lifetime vacations either.

He went to Europe with his parents, to Spain to visit Billy in college and to Jordan on archeological digs. He often went on work-related trips to different cities and states I had never seen, but I always needed to stay home and watch the boys or work.

Not that I blame Bill. This book is not intended to cast blame or put anyone in a bad light, but looking back, I can see where we should have created more "happy memories" and taken time for each other.

I should have demanded. He should have insisted.

When the challenges of life and times became more serious, the family glue might have been stronger.

But, when Philip was an infant and Billy was a small child, Bill was leaving for Europe the next day. I had finished making Bill a light blue sports jacket to wear to the meetings. I had carefully cut the material on the bias. Every step of sewing had been followed with painstaking care. Each piece had been carefully pressed. The buttonholes were perfect. It was a loving gift to him as he got ready to leave.

Bill, on the other hand, had no time for frivolous things. Each day his list of things to do had gotten longer and longer and, as usual, machines broke, cars wouldn't start and dorm kids got into trouble. He was frustrated when I complained about him never being home. He was upset when people did not cooperate with his *list*.

I found his last "to do" list after he left for Europe and copied it into my diary.

*"Bill's unbelievable agenda for his last evening home was relax and read? No. His list included:*

1) *Finish work on the yearbook*
2) *Do some darkroom work*
3) *Run off and staple the Trailblazer*
4) *Wash and wax the car*
5) *Over-haul a lawnmower*
6) *Eat*
7) *Do the worship service in the dorm*
8) *Devotions at bedtime"*

Looking back, I wonder if Bill ever wished his list had been more like:

1) Help Linda with the housework so we can have a special evening together.
2) Walk to the waterfalls with my family.
3) Read a bedtime story to Billy and Philip.
4) Get a dorm monitor and don't answer the door or phone after 8 p.m.
5) Eat a candlelight supper with Linda and the boys.
6) Present Linda and the boys with some "forget-me-not" presents.
7) Have family worship and God Bless each one while I'm gone.

# Chapter 31

## A Dorm Full of Roosters

Slamming the door to the dean's apartment behind him and storming into the living room where I was nursing baby Philip, Neil seemed unusually flustered.

"Better start checking shoes!" he says to Bill as he sat down with a deep sigh not noticing that I was trying to modestly feed the baby.

"What?"

"Yea, shoes!"

"Are they gone?"

"I checked rooms 1 and 5. Room 9 isn't too cool towards me though so I didn't check there."

"Tell me quick. What about shoes?" I demand.

"Well, you see...." But just them Tom Brevig stepped in (without knocking) to discuss the whereabouts of Howie who had been missing for two days from the school campus. It was assumed he had gone to see his girlfriend at the local college in Dayton.

"What's his girlfriend's name at Bryan College? Can we just call and ask for Howie? Or, should we call the girl's dorm? Or, the office?"

I would have enjoyed listening to this conversation and I really was interested in the mystery of the shoes, but a little boy's voice called me from the bedroom where Billy was waking up from a very short nap.

"Mommy, 'ou go work today?" Billy rubbed his still sleepy eyes and reached out for me to hold him and baby Philip too.

"Yes Mommy go to work for a little while and Robin will take you for a walk in the woods. After that I'll be home and we'll make some cookies," I promised.

Sitting my boys in the middle of the living room where several students and Neil were still solving the problems of the school and the world, I hurried to the school cafeteria to get Bill a lunch tray. I made a note to put my uniform in the dryer and start another load of laundry before time to leave for the sanitarium at 2 p.m.

I also needed to check the dormitory rooms of the guys who had failed the morning inspection and give them a pass for lunch. Several were in bed with minor illnesses and would need their temps taken and assured that one day off was sufficient to cure whatever ailed them.

Bang. Bang. Bang. The slamming of the dryer door doesn't bring the usual results, but enough bangs bring Bill who promptly "fixes" it.

"See honey, the piece just fell way down in there. Better find a dryer elsewhere."

By the time Robin arrived, all the male students had gone to their respective assignments. The dorm was quiet. My babies were quiet. Billy was looking forward to a walk in the woods.

I gave Robin a small list of chores to do if she could possibly get to it and headed down the path and across the swinging bridge to the nursing home where I would supervise students giving patient care and I would pass the evening medicines.

During report my supervisor casually mentioned that someone complained because we were bringing the residents to the dining room and starting supper trays too early. This had been a common problem that I thought we had solved months ago.

"No, we do not start serving trays in the dining room before 4:30," I said.

"Well, I thought I'd just throw that out to you."

"But, believe me, we haven't been starting early, " I repeated earnestly.

"Well, I just thought I'd throw that out to you," she said as she eyed the plastic bag I was holding.

"By the way, why aren't you in uniform?"

"I'll have it on in 20 minutes. My dryer broke this afternoon. I thought I'd put it in the san dryer real quick. I'm sorry but there was nothing else to do."

Returning to her report, she told me we had a new admission but the paperwork wasn't complete. I needed to order the liquid medicines from the pharmacy and to "save some spaces" on the nurses notes because she hadn't had time to do her charting. She wanted us to move a resident from Room 14 to Room 18 and we needed to put a siderail on the bed in Room 17.

The Aminophyline for the new patient was in the med room next to the shampoo if he started having an asthma attack.

The patient in 13 would need a suppository at bedtime and could I please find out what happened to the pain pills for the patient in Room 10. She asked if I had given the patient in Room 9 a pain pill last night because he was asking for it "again" and he didn't have any pain medicine ordered.

Horrified, I replied that never in a million years would I do that! I wasn't the only nurse on staff and she had to ask ME if I'd "borrowed" medication from another patient? I thought she knew me better than that.

"Well, I just thought I'd ask," she replied.

She walked away with a reminder not to start supper before 4:30 p.m. and to make the new patient care boy put tape on the taps of his shoes.

I turned to my med cart feeling hopelessly frustrated, her remark also reminding me to ask Neil about the mystery of the shoes.

Suddenly I heard a riding mower in high gear racing around the building. It must be Jim who had been told many times to keep it down around the sanitarium where the noise upsets the residents. By the time I got a window open to yell at him, he was disappearing around the far corner of the building leaving a dust trail in his wake.

Stepping out the front door, I met him at the sidewalk.

"No speeding!"

"Speeding? You call that speeding? I had it in first gear!"

"Yes Jim, I don't care if it has five reverse gears and only one forward gear, if you don't slow it down I'm going to yank the key."

Back inside residents are asking for me and the laundry supervisor is sitting at the desk waiting for me. She says she thinks she is having chest pains. Would I please check her blood pressure? It's 146/62, which is acceptable, so she asks me to check her hemoglobin. That test result is within normal range at 14. Her color is good. Her skin is warm and dry. She's having no trouble breathing so I encourage her to relax while I check on the patient care aides.

I got the girls (and one guy) together for a little report that included the admonishment not to start serving early. Also, one resident was leaving for a doctor appointment in an hour and that meant giving a fighting tiger a bath! I assigned two of my four girls to that task.

Answering the persistent telephone at the nurse's station, I heard a wailing little voice.

"Mommy, 'ou pick up my toys when 'ou come home in a little bit."

"Billy, did Robin ask you to pick up your toys?"

"Yes, but 'ou do it."

"Billy you must mind Robin."

"No Mommy. 'ou do it (tears nearly drown out his voice. 'Ou do it when 'ou get home."

"Billy, if Robin told you to pick up your toys, you must do what she says."

"No Mommy. 'ou will do it. 'ou will do it...."

I say a gentle, "Good-bye Billy" and softly hang up the phone.

It's after 4:00 and the patient care girls suddenly remember they have choir practice after work.

"May we serve early?"

"Absolutely not!"

The phone rings again.

This time it's a reminder that I'm expected to take pictures at Ruthann's baby shower tonight. Also, don't forget to bring the covered dish. Yes, I had remembered the film and Robin was making a macaroni dish.

Dinner finally over, the girls hurried to get their resident in bed so they could leave a few minutes early for their meeting.

As I'm giving the last of the afternoon meds, a young man walks up to me and asks, "Are you in charge?"

Thankful that I'm dressed as a nurse now and wearing my nurses cap, I affirm that I am.

"Is everybody ready?"

"Ready for what?"

"We called earlier today and told the supervisor we'd be in to sing tonight."

Ignoring the grumbling girls, I quickly helped them get the residents back up who would enjoy the program. I would not get out on time tonight and neither would they!

When the night nurse came in I cringed at our disorganization and the work I would have to pass on to her. Mrs. Jones was a kind Christian woman who never complained so it was especially difficult to leave extra work for her to do. She cheerfully took my report and urged me to get back to my "boys".

Back home at the dorm, Billy has finally picked up his toys, placing all his books on the bed next to his pillow. Philip is fussing for his next feeding and Robin is in the middle of what is usually my tidy kitchen.

"Here taste this."

I taste. I gag. I smile. I don't know what's wrong with it, but it doesn't taste like the recipe I left with her! She assures me she followed directions carefully.

Maybe it's not too bad once you get used to the taste. Anyway, it's time to go and I'm not ready. No one can feed Philip but me and I'm headed to the bedroom this time.

"Come on, Billy. I'll read you a book while I feed Philip."

Neil is back and urges me to hurry.

"Hey by the way. What's with the shoes?" I finally ask.

"They're muddy. Somebody's been sneaking out," he answers with a grin.

Baby Philip and little Billy fall asleep while I'm reading to them. Suddenly I'm tired to the bone and realize I'm unwilling to leave my babies tonight.

Bill has to attend a staff meeting and is still somewhere out on campus. I ask Neil to get our friend Floyd Phillips and see if he will take pictures at the shower.

As I rest and relax for a few brief moments, I realize what was wrong with the macaroni dish. Robin has used Fleischmann's yeast instead of brewers yeast! That was what I tasted. I could imagine the dish of food expanding bigger and bigger as it warmed and mixed with the liquid. I could also imagine everyone having to get their stomachs pumped out!

A quick call to the party relieved my mind when Paula assured me they hadn't started eating yet and she would remove the dish from the table.

Yes, tomorrow would bring more challenges but the busy life of a Mother Hen in a dorm of young Roosters was the biggest challenge of all.

We lived at Laurelbrook for the next three years. Soon after Philip was born, we moved to the big city of Chattanooga where I had to plant my own flowers. Where city parks were too dangerous for a young lady to sit and play her flute and where little children had to be kept close to your side.

I missed the mountain laurels at my back door and the chapel in the woods. I worried about the boys in the dorm and wondered about my patients at the nursing home.

But soon we moved on to Nashville where Bill finished his Master's Degree, then Cleveland, Ohio where he worked as a principal for a year and finally to Andrews University at Berrien Springs, Michigan where Bill finally completed his PhD and the boys grew up into young men. Where I thought I would either freeze to death or die from loneliness.

# Angel Nurse

My patients expect an Angel Nurse
When they hurt and feel their worst!
They want the best of care from me.
They want to see a Busy Bee!
Meds on time and pain pills too
A smile that's positively true!
Please give me Angel Wings
To answer quickly when they ring.
Angel wisdom when they ask,
"How long is this going to last?"
Steady hands and eyes to see
When I have to start that next IV.
I ask not for wealth, nor praise I seek.
Just a boost of strength when I am weak.
Patients getting well and going home
Back to Family and talking on the phone.
Will they remember at setting Sun?
The Nurse whose work is never done.

~Linda Meikle (2004)

# Chapter 32

## A Good Nurse on a Bad Day

It's almost 2 a.m. and I still have a Herald-Palladium story to write. I wonder if there's any way possible to get this story straight and keep it interesting for the reader. If not, my editor will be calling for me to rewrite it!

My little dog, Muffy, jumps into my lap and begs for some attention. It was a long evening without her master. Sometimes after a busy hospital shift when nothing went right, and no one waits to greet me when I get home, a tiny little dog can be life's greatest reward.

"Only ten patients. That shouldn't be too bad," I note at the beginning of my shift. The last time I had 12 and did ok. (Once my load was 16 and I refuse to do that again!")

After a lengthy shift report that includes more information about what didn't get done than facts about my patients, I set out to make quick rounds, introduce myself and do initial assessments.

My first patient is lying in bed with an IV infusing in his arm. He is muttering to himself. Wanting to assess his orientation I ask, "Hi. Do you know where you are?"

I expect a blank look and the mumbling to continue but suddenly he rises up, looks me square in the eye and yells,

"Of course I know where the hell I am! What I want to know is where is my doctor? He said I could go home by 4 p.m.!"

Assuring him I will try to find out about his discharge, and realizing that his IV would have to be removed before he walks out the front door, I look over at his roommate.

A jolly old man with one leg says he is just fine. "I'm sure, honey, you'll change my bandage soon. It hasn't been done all day. And, no hurry but if you have time, will you bring me a pain shot?"

The dressing on his stump is soiled with a dirty green and yellow stain that comes from an infection. I detect a foul odor indicating it had been quite awhile since it has been cleaned. The doctor's orders are to clean his stump wound three times a day! Smiling reassuringly, I promise the shot and the treatment soon.

The next patient is in a VIP room. The orders are to turn and position every one hour (not every two), frequent suctioning of a tracheotomy and to force fluids.

The lady is drowning in her own fluids! I grab the suction tube, remove the inner catheter of the trach and suck out the accumulation of phlegm that is cutting off her airway.

She smiles with appreciation as she takes a deep breath and clasps my hand in hers. I turn up the oxygen to the proper liters and slowly back out of the room. She badly needs trach care but that is a complicated process that I cannot do right now.

It is always hard for me to understand why patients requiring the most observation are often admitted to a private room where less caregivers can monitor their care!

Next down the hall is an old lady from the local nursing home with a broken hip. She is a recent post-op to repair the hip, but the doctor has just ordered her to be "out of bed" with no weight bearing on the affected leg.

The woman does not respond to my greeting although her eyes are open. She lies immobile with a large pillow taped in place holding her legs apart. She looks stiff and smells like she has a soiled diaper. The edges of her mouth are yellow from eggs that dribbled when she was fed.

The water pitcher on the bedside table is empty and the call light is lying on the floor. Has anyone called family members to sit with her? Or, would someone come yelling at me later on because "grandma" doesn't talk to them.

The two elderly women in Room 222 are in a good mood and ready to make the hospital their home. An IV tubing hangs limply beside bed A. In report the nurse said the IV had infiltrated during the night and no one had been able to find another vein. Would we please try?

Bed two is getting blood and it is dripping slowly as prescribed. The paperwork at her bedside should have contained vital signs every 15 minutes but nothing has been charted since an hour before.

At least she isn't showing any signs of a reaction to the blood. She isn't having chills or running a fever. Her breathing is fine and she has no redness at the IV site.

Room 223 is also a VIP but I don't know why. He's a recent post-op and I hear him cussing and swearing very angrily at someone. As I near the room, I realize that he is in isolation because there's an Isolation Cart next to his door. I wonder why it wasn't mentioned in report! Isolation procedures are the same, so I slip on the gown, gloves and mask and enter the hostile room.

"My doctor promised me I wouldn't have any pain! I'm gonna sue him! Nurse, this is unbelievable. Just unbelievable! That no good … doctor! Go get me a pain shot right now and don't be lazy about it!"

I'm obligated to go find out about this patient. A quick review of the chart finds that the isolation has been discontinued. The order, written that morning, is scribbled across the page, "Take this man off isolation. He is not infectious!"

The progress notes indicate there are "shadows" on his chest x-ray but no information about what he has. The charge nurse ignores my concern with the comment, "If he coughs or sneezes, you aren't protected by that little mask anyway."

The nurses' notes indicate that he had a pain shot just before change of shift and can't have another one for two hours! I hate having to tell him that.

In room 224, I find a pleasant lady who had exploratory surgery two days ago. We know they found invasive cancer but her doctor hasn't told her yet. The family is waiting for the doctor to come in today. Everyone is trying to be optimistic and positive and cheerful while waiting for the bad news to be given by her doctor.

Room 228 (why can't they at least keep my rooms all together?) is an older man who just returned from surgery for an aneurysm.

His pain shots are causing him to be confused and combative. He thinks he's in Vietnam and he is stronger than a mule!

His wrists strain against the wrist restraints and the bed rails rattle with his thrashing. I'm afraid he will tear out the stitches – inside his chest where the artery was repaired and on the outside holding his skin together!

The charge nurse said she will get an order for something else to sedate him but so far the doctor has not called back.

Room 230 is a new admit, but I haven't gotten report on him because he arrived during shift report. He was a "direct admit" from the doctor's office. I guess they think we don't need report on those patients. The charge nurse said he has congestive heart failure but was in no distress.

It's time to start the 4 p.m. routine med pass and catch up on pain shots. Each medication will have to be checked against the medication book and every pill given will need an initial that I gave it.

All shots of Insulin will have to be double checked with another nurse and every narcotic pain med will be signed out on the narcotic book and charted in the nurses' notes. I will have to indicate if the shot was effective and if it wasn't, I will have to call the doctor for new orders.

A reoccurring nightmare is that I am at work in my slip because I forgot to put on my uniform and during my shift I have forgotten to pass the meds. After reading this chapter, I think you will understand why I have that bad dream.

Suddenly I hear the public address overhead calling a Code Blue.

"Code Blue Room 224. Code Blue Room 224. Code Blue Room 224."

That's my patient whose family is waiting for the doctor!

Before I can snap the med cart locked, there is a stream of staff sprinting toward the room.

The stairwell door bursts open and the ER doctor yells, "What's the history on this patient?"

Grabbing the patient's chart, I try to remember what I've heard in report and my observations earlier.

Neither seems like much to give in response to the two-second silence while everyone waits for me to answer the doctor.

"Fresh exploratory post-op," I yell so everyone will know she's a recent surgery, could have cancer and she might have thrown a blood clot.

I'm glad to see the respiratory technician with an ambu bag giving respirations so I don't have to do mouth-to-mouth but no one has started compressions while the EKG leads are being attached to her chest.

I grab the backboard from the crash cart and someone lifts the mattress so it can be wedged under the top half of her body.

Someone else ushers the family out of the room and out of the way. The room is already crowded with the entire Code Team who is always prepared for any Code Blue called in the hospital.

They come as a team from the ER, the ICU and various hospital departments. Any doctor who is in the hospital is required to respond.

Climbing onto the bed to kneel beside the apparently lifeless body I find the correct hand position and start counting with each compression remembering that each downstroke must compress the sternum at least 1 and ½ inches.

I find that I'm instantly exhausted because her body pushes down into the mattress and the monitor doesn't show good cardiac compressions! I push harder and grunt each count. "One-and, Two-and, Three-and"

Someone places a red hat on the doctor in charge of the code and he yells for an IV medication. An experienced ICU nurse immediately starts pushing the med into an IV line that another MD has quickly but effortless started.

"Give 300 jolts and stand back," the head doctor orders.

I jump down from the bed and lean over to catch my breath.

No response.

A young, strong male "code nurse" takes over with compressions and I thank him with my eyes.

I note that we have a scribe writing down each step of the code and the second hand of the code clock is running. It's been two minutes.

My hands are bloody from the open incision. I had forgotten about the incision as I started compressions.

The code is running smoothly if it can be said that way. But the patient is not responding. I know it will be "called" in a few minutes. I need to get the family prepared for this news but I must go wash my hands first!

It's not difficult to identify the husband, but it's very hard to look him in the eye.

"The doctor will want to talk to you soon," I say gently.

"Let me show you the waiting room."

"Is she going to be ok? When can I see her?' he asks.

"Soon", I reply with a heavy heart.

The doctor mutters that he thinks she threw a blood clot that killed her instantly.

My other patients are waiting and some not so patiently!

A patient with his backside showing through the wide break in his hospital gown is getting onto the elevator. There are blood drops on the floor where he has pulled out his IV. I run to catch him but the elevator door slams shut in my face. This is the man who was waiting for his doctor to discharge him! I quickly call security to catch him at the front door.

Behind me I hear a timid female voice calling me. It's the wife from the man in 223 who was cussing out his doctor and demanding a pain shot.

"Please come. He wants you right now. My husband really needs a pain shot. Did you get it yet?"

To my great relief, the charge nurse tells me that she got an order for a one-time pain shot of Demerol 100 mg. and he could have it now.

Not looking to see if she had actually written the order, I quickly pull it from the narcotic drawer and hurry to his room. He also takes his afternoon meds for high blood pressure and his antibiotic pills.

The new admission hasn't demanded attention but I know that his doctor will be in expecting his orders to be noted and a nurse to follow him to examine the patient.

The constant beeping of an IVAC machine alerts me that blood had run in and the empty container must soon be returned to the lab. Hopefully the aide has taken the required vital signs.

The unit clerk tells me I have a phone call from my husband. I tell her to tell him I'll call back.

Entering the new admission's room, I recognize his illness by the sound of his breathing. He's short of breath and his lips are blue and the oxygen running at 2 liters. His barrel-shaped chest and pursed lip breathing are indicative of COPD. He's 86 years old and I smell the odor of cigarettes.

He has chronic obstructive pulmonary disease (COPD) from smoking all his life! He's still sneaking a smoke even with his oxygen on and orders on the door for no smoking.

The charge nurse has given me the entire set (4 pages) of admission paperwork to do even though she (as the RN) is supposed to complete her section.

I'm confident of this patient's diagnosis but I ask anyway because it's on the paperwork.

"Why are you sick?"

"I got this pain in my leg and I can't walk," he replies.

Surprised at his answer, I tell him I need to examine him.

"Let me check you over. Let's get you into a hospital gown," I explain as I help him unbuckle his belt and drop his pants.

I control a silent gasp as I notice that his scrotum is holding half his intestines. There is no penis in sight!

He wears a dirty smelly truss that he doesn't want me to touch.

"I wear this all the time," he says as he holds it tightly.

Just then, there a persistent tap at the door and my aide beacons for me to step out into the hall.

"The trach lady is dead," she says in deadpan.

"The charge nurse says I have to clean her up for the morgue but I've never touched a dead person before."

Now there are tears in her eyes and desperation in her voice.

"Well, just close the door and put a 'Please see the nurse before entering' sign on her door," I instruct.

Two deaths on one shift is unusual but not unheard of. Now two of my patients have died. It's like that in a hospital. One must adjust to change all the time!

I assume my trach patient was a "no code" but I feel sad that she is gone. I hope she didn't choke to death because the trach got plugged!

Just then the COPD patient's doctor comes into the room and says, "What's wrong with my patient?"

"You admitted him with CHF (congestive heart failure) but I think he has a strangulated hernia," I reply.

"Oh well, I had to admit him with something. It doesn't matter what. Have him ready for surgery in an hour." He turns and walks out the door without even a hello to his patient.

I still have meds to pass. Charts to open. IV's running dry. Dressings to change.

I have two dead bodies. One will lay in repose for the family to gather around and say goodbye. I'll call the funeral home when they have left.

The other body has no family and will be taken to the hospital morgue after we have cleaned her up.

Right now, the surgery patient has to have STAT blood work, STAT chest x-ray, an EKG, a surgical permit signed and IV started

There is an order for a urine specimen that I can't obtain because I can't find a penis to insert the catheter into!

By now everything is hopelessly off schedule. The surgeon is standing at the nurses' station asking when his patient will be ready.

"What have you girls been doing the last hour?" he asks impatiently.

He says he will get the urine specimen in surgery and I breathe a sigh of relief.

I hand him the completed four-page assessment to read and hurry past him to take care of my other patients.

The aide tells me that the man in Room 223 has just thrown up all over his bed.

She isn't going to get the hip patient out of bed unless they send an orderly up to help.

She isn't going into either of the rooms to help get the bodies cleaned up, and she's going to supper now!

The unit clerk tells me that my editor from the newspaper has called and left a reminder that my story is due tonight and he will be working late at the newspaper office waiting for the story.

As I clean up the emesis and fume because I now have to do the aides work too, the patient's wife gives away a secret with her comment.

"Demerol always does that," she states.

Yes, she's a nurse but she isn't helping me with her husband!

The patient wants another pain shot because he "threw-up" the last one!

Surgery is here to pick up their "strangulated hernia" for the operating room.

"Could you please put a nameband on him? He doesn't have one," a clean sweet-smiling nurse asks.

I wonder how in the world he's gotten all the pre-op testing done without a nameband. There's one on his chart with the admission paperwork that I should have put on his wrist when I filled out the forms.

I hurry to double check his name, as one must do before surgery.

"Hi Leonard. I just need to double check your name so we can put the tag on for surgery".

He gets wild! "My name is not Leonard. I've lived here 75 years. Everybody in this town knows my name is Ray. Where in the world did you get Leonard?"

Surgery waits while I pick up the phone in the room. Everything in the computer and admitting has to be changed! I hear the clerk moan in exasperation as if this is my fault.

The surgeon finishes reading the assessment and says, "Hey, this is pretty darn good, Linda." It's probably the first one he's ever read!

Now the morgue tech is here to pick up the body for the hospital morgue. I know it will take smooth talking to keep him from getting impatient while I clean up the patient. Thank goodness there are no family members waiting to say goodbye.

As I carefully and tenderly wash her body, I apologize for not being there when she needed someone.

Finally, we are ready to transfer her body to the morgue cart. I ask where the second orderly is because it's difficult to slide a dead person from a soft bed up higher to the cart. The morgue tech shrugs and says they are short staffed too.

We look out the door for anyone who might be willing to help but there's no one in sight except the surgeon and we don't dare ask him.

Shaking my head and rolling my eyes, we tighten the sheet around her large body and count, "1-2-3- PULL" as we drag body from bed to cart.

The body drops to the floor with a heavy thud! We stand there feeling mortified! We can't think of absolutely anybody to call. This has never happened to either of us before and we are terrified that someone might walk in now!

Somehow with every ounce of superhuman strength and fortitude not to get caught in this mess, we get the lady on the flimsy cart and vow to never tell a soul what just happened.

I turn to my medicine cart and refuse to stop for anything or anyone until all the shift meds are passed out and pain shots are given!

The charge nurse is in the med room crying because a doctor yelled at her for calling him at home.

Aides are wearily making last rounds and everybody is exhausted, hungry and in need of a potty break.

It's 10:45 p.m. and I WILL work overtime tonight finishing up my charting after the night nurses get here to take over our shift. Nights will complain that I left them work to do and treatments not done. I will have to endure the comment, "And you had only eight patients?"

The unit clerk has left several notes for me because she knows I can't take time for messages. Grandma Mascunana wants milk by morning. Philip wants to know where his Steelers shirt is. Billy wants to spend the night with Todd. The editor went home and will expect the story to be on his desk by 7 a.m. Bill says they had a great time at the game. What game?

Later, driving home in the winter darkness and feeling a bit sorry for myself I can't believe the flashing red and blue lights I see in my rearview mirror. Pulling over and blinking back tears as the police officer's flashlight blinds me, I wonder what I have done wrong. I had been driving very carefully on the slightly slippery road.

"Did you know your bright lights are on and you didn't dim them for on coming traffic?"

"I tried, sir, but the button won't work." (This was when the bright light button was on the floorboard.)

"Would you get out of the car, ma'am!"

That night I had the bad fortune to meet a very hot headed Berrien Springs' police officer who refused to allow me to drive the rest of the way home.

In a white nurse's uniform, wearing no coat on a cold winter night, he forced me to walk along the highway for almost a mile to my house.

At home, there's a note on the table to call the editor and call grandma about a doctor's appointment early in the morning. The boys and my husband are sleeping.

Muffy jumps on my lap and begs for some attention. Sometimes after a busy hospital shift when nothing went right and no one waits to greet me when I get home, a tiny little dog can be life's greatest reward.

*Philip with little Taffy*

# Chapter 33

## *Too Many Hats*

Last Thursday Philip was hit by a car while collecting for his newspaper route while I was sitting at a school board meeting taking notes for the local newspaper.

I wear so many hats these days sometimes they get mixed up. Sometimes they won't all fit at the same time, and sometimes it's difficult knowing which one to put on!

Billy is 14 going on 21. He just graduated from a paper route to tossing hamburgers at the local mini-golf course after school. Philip is 11 and just starting his first job with as a newspaper carrier. Both are taking piano lessons. Daily practice sessions and newspaper routes consume most every afternoon and each needs a mother's touch – or at least adult supervision or substitute as the need arises.

I'm working at the hospital as a nurse and running after every newsworthy event 24/7 as the newspaper reporter for our town.

Bill is working many hours every day at the university trying to climb the ladder of success and complete his PhD before the boys are old enough to start their own degree program.

Most every day Grandma Mascunana, who lives in a nearby retirement home, demands some attention, a trip to the store or a doctor's appointment.

So, when a car backed into Philip on his bike, he was more frightened than hurt and asked the police to get his mom from the school board meeting. The chief of police came to the door of the boardroom and motioned for me to step out.

He assured me Philip was more frightened than hurt. He said he consoled Philip by telling him, "I know your mother. She took my picture for the paper."

A quick trip to the emergency room (back then one could make a "quick trip" to the ER), checked out Philip with only a few bumps and scrapes but the doctor detected a "stuttering heartbeat" that would need further tests at a later time.

Back at home the pampering began. Ice cream, computer games, friends over, no chores, and later then usual lights-out time. Philip enjoyed a rare moment in the sunshine of pampering thanks to his mom's relief that he was okay and guilt that I wasn't there when he needed me!

Billy gave notice that he wasn't going to take over Philip's paper route for a week. "I'm not doing the paper route next week and no one can make me. I already have a job," he announced.

On Friday, I didn't go to work at the hospital. It was one of the rare times that I actually called off from work. Philip had an appointment for the cardiologist to check out his heart. It was also Friday, and nothing was ready for Sabbath.

As a Seventh-day Adventist, people will expect my house to be "Sabbath Clean" by sundown. Church clothes need to be washed and pressed. Sabbath dinner still needs to be prepared. I was up until almost daylight writing the school board story for the paper after all the accident action settled down and everybody was finally in bed.

There are rare moments when I stop and give myself a pat on the back and say, "Thank-you, Linda." Others seem to take me for granted to be there when they need me, to have an answer for every question and to have everything done at the right time and place.

Sabbath morning as I hit the snooze button, I realized with a start that I had to play my flute for Sabbath School. Something else was buzzing in my head too. Oh yes, there had been a big barn fire during the night and the fire tones had gone out on the scanner for Berrien Springs to respond with mutual aid to Sodus Fire Department.

I'm usually out the door with my camera bag over my shoulder before the final fire tones are ending. But last night the fire was out of my area, so I had called my editor at home first to verify that a reporter was needed. He had said I didn't need to go!

We had an agreement that if I went out of my area at night, I would call my editor at home to confirm another correspondent wasn't in route and to alert him to the breaking news so he wouldn't hear it first on the radio on his way to work!

At church my flute solo went well, but I became alarmed when I found a pamphlet inserted into our church bulletin urging the church members to vote against a proposed horseracing track to be built near our town.

Putting on my Newspaper Reporter Hat, I grumbled all the way home. Tom would want a story on this. Pamphlets in every church? Both Saturday and Sunday churches! I would have to call and talk to the pastor of every church in town, and there were at least 15 churches in Berrien Springs!

"Get the story for Monday's paper," the editor said. "Find out if the churches are putting pressure on their members to vote against the race track!"

As we sat down to a quiet Sabbath home-cooked dinner, my mind was whirling with ideas. (None of which I was suppose to do during the Sabbath hours.)

I needed to call the township supervisor, the village president, proposers of the track, and the Sunday pastors before I left for work in a couple hours! I'd have to call the Saturday ministers on Sunday!

Quickly but quietly, I called my friends at the other SDA churches in town and confirmed that each of the other SDA churches had slipped those pamphlets into their church bulletins.

I left messages for the Sunday pastors to call me but was worried to discover that many of them were on vacation and I would have to get answers from the head elders or other church members left in charge.

By then, it was almost 2:30 p.m. and time to be on the road for the hospital so I wouldn't be late for report!

Returning late that night after a usual hectic shift at the hospital, I collected the messages on my answering machine and made an outline for the story that would have to be completed within 24 hours. Thankfully, there were no accident or fire calls during the night.

By almost daybreak on Sunday morning I was at the construction site of the All-Nations SDA church to find out who was the spokesperson while that pastor was on vacation. I was instructed that I would locate that person in his garden but when I arrived there, his wife said he too was out of town. She directed me to his secretary for a statement on the racetrack matter.

It's time for my family to be up because they're leaving for Chicago for a ball game at 11 a.m. At home Bill says, "Pick up a newspaper while you're running around."

"Mom, where's my White Sox hat?'

"Where are my jeans with the wrinkles?"

"What's for breakfast?"

"Grandma called and said she needs to go to the store this morning."

By 12:30 I'm sitting down to write but I feel like a pressure cooker about to explode and I can hardly breathe. I'm beginning to wonder if this was all a stupid waste of time. No one appreciates a snoopy newspaper reporter – especially one asking for comments on such a sensitive issue. I've listened to many arguments today but no one was willing to take responsibility for a comment "on the record".

Preachers have given me mini-sermons on the belief of their particular church. Citizens have argued at me like I was the person who proposed the racetrack. (I also interviewed him. He's the local veterinarian.) I've spent hours smiling, nodding and listening while gently prodding for the answers to my questions about who started the campaign to put pamphlets in the church bulletins.

I file the story at 2:05 p.m. and eat a cold fried egg left over from breakfast. The Sunday newspaper is scattered all over the living room. Breakfast dishes are still on the table. Sabbath clothes lay where they were dropped on the floor yesterday. There's not a clean or dry towel in the bathroom. There's no water in the dog dish. The light is blinking on the answering machine.

Rushing out the door in time to stop for gas on the way to work, I arrived at the medical floor and found myself in a different world.

People are being admitted. Call lights are beeping. Patients want cold water in their water pitcher. They demand pain shots they've waited hours for. Some are confused and falling out of bed. One or two of my patents are dying and family members look at me with sorrowful eyes as if they think I can stop the inevitable.

A doctor asks if I can make rounds with him and I can't say no even though the charge nurse should do that, but she is on a supper break. Another nurse reminds me it's my night to check the crash cart as I double check an Insulin shot with her. Overhead I hear my name being paged to the desk for a phone call.

Tom has a question about the story and wants more quotes. He says there's a report of a bad car accident in Berrien Springs that I'll need to follow up on when I get off work.

The unit secretary gives me a note that says my husband and the kids are back from the game. The note also indicates there's been a bad car accident in town. A lady was killed. There's also a message from the Lutheran Pastor who wants to change his story about the racetrack.

Just then there's an emergency in Room 233. A patient seems to be choking and we all run to help, but it's only a post-op tracheal spasm that quickly passes. I reassure the family that once in a while this happens after surgery from the endotracheal tube.

By shift's end eight hours later, I'm hungry, tired and my feet hurt so bad I can't wait to take off my shoes when I get into the car.

At home all is quiet as everyone is worn out from the game and the long trip to Chicago. There's one piece of cheese pizza left in the open box on the table. I'm surprised the dog didn't steal it! I talk to myself as I put it into the microwave. Just then the phone rings! It's 12:15 p.m. and I glance at the scanner. IT'S TURNED OFF!

I grab the phone before the second ring. I wonder what emergency is happening that I've missed again.

But it's Tom, still at the newspaper office trying to put the paper to bed. Knowing I'd be arriving home about now, he wanted to tell me that my story is going to make the front page. "Thanks for a great job!" Someone else will get the fatal PI story.

The dog at my feet takes a deep sigh in his sleep. I can go to sleep now too.

# Chapter 34

## _Catastrophic Diagnosis_

I had gone to the doctor's office in tears. I had left in distress, filled with dread and worry. At 35-years of age I had just been informed that within 15 years rheumatoid arthritis could have me incapacitated as an invalid.

It was not so difficult for me to believe. My great-grandmother, Grandma Padgett, had been left confined to her bed at an early age with her fingers bent into her hands, her legs drawn up and useless and her back bowed and stiff. I had helped take care of her as a small child when we lived in Avon Park.

Bill had not gone to this medical appointment with me even though my joints were so stiff and painful that he sometimes had to help me get dressed when painful hands refused to work little buttons or pull the zipper at the back of my dress. With frustrating yowls of pain, I had to ask for help with simple things!

He knew I often complained that my elbows felt like they had nails pounded through them and my knees were increasingly stiff. The pain was making it difficult to walk any distance, get up from a chair or in and out of a car. Because I seemed in otherwise good health, we figured I was too young to have anything serious. But the pain told me otherwise! Grandma's beatings, the overturned wagon accident on Carver Creek, three serious car accidents since then, the constant stress and family heredity, all contributed to the causes for the crippling discomfort now.

I felt overwhelmed with grief as I got into the car and headed toward the quiet solitude of the Lake Michigan County Park where I sometimes rested for a few moments of quietness, or took the boys to play on the beach when the weather was nice. (The same area where my youngest son proposed to his wife many years later!)

Vowing not to give in to this disease and setback in my life, my thoughts turned to actions I needed to take in order to get myself in better health. The doctor had cautioned that stress can aggravate any medical problem and he had encouraged me to slow down and take time for myself. I reviewed the horrible schedule I was keeping.

There never seemed to be enough money to pay all the bills and, as a nurse, I could always work one more shift to get us through one more paycheck. That's not to say that Bill wasn't working many hours too, but he was on salary so it was more difficult for him to contribute.

At one point, we had gone into a venture with his parents raising cherry tomatoes on their small farm. We planted, cultivated, picked, sorted, packed and took cherry tomatoes to market all summer. In order to be available to help with the tomatoes, I was working the night shift at a local hospital, but I only half rested and hardly ever slept during the day.

Others saw the damage this was doing to our marriage and me and, on at least one occasion, our pastor took Bill aside and cautioned him that he needed to, "take better care of Linda." But Bill could see no way out and had no solution to change things. He depended on his mother to help us out of each major financial emergency.

Remembering how chiropractic adjustments had helped when I had sciatic pain down my legs as a teenager at Laurelbrook, I wondered if using the natural approach would help me now.

Most chiropractors will explain how manipulating the spine to open the nervous pathways from the spinal cord to all parts of the body will allow the natural healing to take place. Much like cleaning a wound to promote good circulation.

There didn't seem to be very many possibilities for changing the stress at home, but getting regular chiropractic adjustments was one action I was going to take right away.

That is how I met Chiropractor "Doc" Stowe. Someone told me about a local chiropractor who practiced out of a small basement office on the main street of our town. As I pulled up beside a door that led down a small flight of steps, I wondered how someone with a bad back would make it to the adjustment table at all!

But the pretty young lady at the desk was efficient and businesslike as she got me registered not only for treatment but also for the educational classes to explain what chiropractic is all about and why one needs regular adjustments.

Doc Stowe, tall, skinny and smiling through a goatee that I thought made him look like the devil, took several x-rays followed by a back-crackling adjustment. The appointment ended with a big hug and "near perfect" wishes for the day!

I wasn't sure of the hug but thought near perfect was a goal to work toward!

So, I started a course of treatments and education about chiropractic care. It is common for spinal adjustments to be started at three times a week – something most people and insurance companies are shocked to discover. Then it is recommended that the body be kept in healthy alignment with twice monthly or monthly appointments.

Healing is not instant but sometimes the effects of an adjustment can be felt immediately. Most of the time, one finds that over time, medical issues improve as the body sends good impulses and blood supply to affected areas.

Doc Stowe, like many entrepreneurs who practice chiropractic medicine, was enthusiastic about the chiropractic cause but he was also cocky with a devil-may-care attitude. Sometimes I was uncomfortable with his flirtatious nature but I noticed that all his patients received the same flagrant, unabashed attention.

His daughter, Kimberly, worked hard to keep the office organized and appointments maintained because her father was the first to admit he was not a good administrator or businessperson! His passion was deer hunting and the year-long preparations for the annual hunting season. His patients knew that the office would be closed for most of the deer-hunting season not only in Michigan but also in Texas and Ohio with chiropractic buddies.

Within a few months, I found that the joint pains were less severe and my stomach didn't hurt so often. After about a year, I could function almost normally again and sometimes many months would pass between treatments. Painful joints, stomach aches and back pain would remind me to head back to Doc Stowe's office for treatment.

During these few years as a patient, I was unaware that his wife had passed away after a long illness or that his daughter's newborn baby had suddenly died from a silent cardiac condition. I was on my own life's course of a marriage falling apart and trying to keep sane in a busy world of working mother with growing teenage boys!

Thankful for a reprieve from the devastating diagnosis, my life resumed to almost pain free days and with new hope to grow old with confidence and good health.

# Chapter 35

## All In a Day's Work

Avoiding my warm cozy bed after getting the boys off to school, I hurried to sort the laundry and start picking up people-clutter around the house. A few minutes of quiet time in the morning is usually the most I get in any given 24-hour period. "It shouldn't be wasted on work that never gets done," I thought.

The home was as sparkling as time allowed and the endless pile of laundry was almost all dry as I hurried off to the hospital for my 3 p.m. – 11 p.m. shift.

The off-going shift was so busy they didn't even see us come in. No one had signed out narcotics for the day so we couldn't start the narcotic count. None of the day nurses had stopped to do their shift charting and everyone was griping about being short-staffed and being too busy to take a break.

Consoling myself that I was more organized than most with my homemade nurse report sheet, and handing a copy to my co-worker who was never organized, we sat down at the long table for the change-of-shift report.

During the slow-paced report from tired nurses who had not sat in a chair for over eight hours, I noted that I had the maximum quota of 12 patients – none of which I had taken care of before! Those 12 included several post-ops and some nursing home patients who would require almost total care. They would need turning every two hours, feeding, diaper changes and comprehensive charting for Medicare regulations.

There was one unusual case that drew my attention. The sister of one of our night nurses was in for 24-hour observation for,

168

"acute anxiety reaction". Before the night was over, I would learn much from this lady about how an overloaded mind works.

Hurrying out to make the initial round of my patients, I noticed that my patient in Room 235 who had gone to Kalamazoo for tests had not returned. Most patients were usually back from outside tests before shift change and always before report was over.

This patient was in for a seizure disorder and the day nurse had forgotten to send his seizure medication with him! It would be vital to watch for his return and to give his meds before he had another seizure!

By the time I had checked most of my patients, I 'd heard so many comments from the staff about the patient in Room 244 with the anxiety reaction that I didn't want to go into that room.

"You'll never get out of there if you go in. She wants you to sit and read the Bible to her, to rub her back and listen to the endless story of how her father is dying in Ann Arbor," the aides warned.

The afternoon went by much too fast. It was hard to keep up with the demands for pain shots, routine medications, bedpans to empty, call lights to answer, dressings to change and doctors who wanted immediate attention.

"I've been waiting for hours!", my patients would complain when I answered call lights the aides should have gotten.

About 8 p.m., I hurriedly grabbed a candy bar and soda pop from the vending machine because the hospital cafeteria had closed hours ago. My mind was busy with a running checklist of things needing my attention. IV's were running dry, surgical patients must be ambulated in the hall and pain shots would be in demand again. The charge nurse stuck her head into the break room to inform me I was getting a new admission.

The new patient had a blood sugar of over 500 – fatal for some people. "She belongs in the unit," I grumbled.

Unable to avoid Room 244 – I slipped into an unreal world of anxiety overload.

"Oh, are you my nurse? I'm so glad it's you. I'm really not crazy. Please don't leave me. Help me to the bathroom and stay with me. Would you please rub my back," and she dropped her gown and leaned over – arms dangling down in front of her. "I'm leaving in the morning to help take care of my dad," she informed me.

I was told that her husband was on his way from Florida and would be in about 8 p.m. Her father had just passed away at a hospital in Ann Arbor and she had spent the last two weeks at his bedside in the Intensive Care Unit.

She thought if she could be there and smile and say pleasant things, her father would not die. But he had taken his last breath when she left him for a moment to answer the phone. Now it was pitiful to see her blame herself for his death one minute and speak as if he was still alive the next.

I had to leave her with her thoughts. The new admission was coming up from the emergency room and I couldn't find an IV pump. It was the hospital policy to keep Insulin drips on a pump, but there was never enough to go around and impossible to find one in a hurry.

The charge nurse was busy too but took a minute to call the supervisor and tell her we HAD to get more help. I asked her if she would please call the doctor for a sedative for the woman in 244.

Suddenly I heard a very loud angry voice at the nurses' station demanding to know what "dirty job" we had for her to do. She was our extra help. I happened to catch the sarcastic comment as I dashed through to grab another IV bag, two pain pills and the Insulin.

By 10 p.m. I hadn't opened my charts or done the paperwork on the new admission. The night nurses would want report on time so they could start their shift, and the supervisor would fuss about any nurse who needed overtime pay to get her work done. It's hard not to snap at slow moving aides or co-workers who are taking another cigarette break!

The intercom calls me to the front desk for a phone call as my patient stumbles during his first walk after surgery.

I'm hungry. I'm tired. My uniform is too tight, and Bill says the boys are skateboarding after dark again.

This is where the handy Nurse Report form helps me finish my shift. Everything I've done that has to be recorded in the charts has been neatly but hastily noted on my sheet for each patient. Closing the last chart as the first 11-7 nurse walks in, I say, "Time's up! Welcome to our world," and head off to report. Tomorrow is another day.

# Chapter 36

## *Circle of Love*

The phone rang while I was mixing a batch of chocolate chip cookies for my boys and their friends coming over to watch a football game on TV. Wiping the sprinkles of flour off my fingers, I answered with my usual cherry, "Helloooo. This is Linda."

"Come quick! Mr. Black just busted the living room window with a chair and he's in the kitchen looking for a knife. He's real upset and won't listen to any of us."

My first response was a quick call to 911 for emergency assistance. As I dashed out the door giving, "finish the cookies" instructions to Philip, I rushed the few blocks to my job at Teresa's County Home where an irate elderly gentleman had suddenly become unmanageable and dangerous at the assisted living facility.

It was my responsibility as the Health Care Administrator to maintain order and answer all calls, medical or otherwise for three assisted living homes in our town. The owner had designated me as her Administrator for the 40-bed facilities after I had worked as her staff nurse for a few years. We had developed a trusting professional relationship while she trained me for the position and monitored my ability to follow her lead before she and her family relocated to Florida.

Now it was my task to keep the other residents and staff of this 20-bed home safe from the outburst of a confused Alzheimer's patient, and it would take delicate persuasive action on my part to see that the combative resident was not taken to jail, but to a medical facility where he could get proper assessment and treatment for his extreme confusion and agitation.

By the time I arrived, the police had the resident in handcuffs and in the back seat of the police car. A burly policeman had thrown a blanket over the man to subdue him. The shattered glass from the window glittered in the flashing red and blue police emergency lights. It appeared there would be no question where this confused elderly man would sleep that night.

I was relieved to see that the Chief of Police had responded to the emergency call and as he stepped out of his car, I followed beside him.

"Hey Jim. Guess your guys have to take this man to jail and lock him up?"

"Well, Hi Linda. Do you have a better plan?"

"As a matter of fact, I do. How about the psyche unit at Memorial Hospital? It's only a few blocks from the jail. I could call and get a direct admit order for you."

The chief agreed that this irate man, now sitting calmly as if he remembered nothing of the past few minutes, would benefit far more with medical attention at the hospital but he explained that if the police took him anywhere, it would have to be to jail.

"I'll take him in my car," I offered, thinking quickly.

"That's not very safe. I don't think you should take a chance of him going off again," Jim countered.

"Well, how about one of your reserves ride with me?" I suggested.

"I guess we could arrange that," Jim said as he glanced over at Ric, one of his best reserves.

With all the legal issues mollified and thanking Jim for working with me on this one, I set off for a long night at the hospital. The chocolate chip cookies would be all gone and the game long over before I got back to my kitchen.

Since taking this job for Teresa's Country Homes, there was never a dull moment in my life. The training classes Teresa sent me to had been very helpful in understanding dementia and Alzheimer's disease. She had also provided management courses and I had spent many months under her tutoring learning her high standards and the professional skills needed to assure the smooth running of these well-respected homes that provided around the clock care for the elderly residents of our town.

The largest 20-bed home was staffed with a supervisor and several aides day and night. A secure fence surrounded the well-kept yard. The gate was locked with a secret code to keep residents in and allowed staff and family unlimited access. All the facilities were exceptionally clean and maintained as home-like as possible.

Teresa had created detailed instructions for every aspect of running an assisted living facility – from menus and recipes for each meal to details on how to clean the stove on a regular schedule. The homes were run like clockwork and rarely got any citations when surveyed by state officials. It was one of the most rewarding jobs I had ever worked, but I had learned to anticipate the unexpected.

For instance, Mr. Black was a new admission this morning. When his daughter brought him to the home located on the main road, she had been impressed with the homelike appearance, family pictures on the walls, well trained staff, home cooked meals and friendly atmosphere. The other residents were clean and well groomed. Activities were going on in the family room and the porches that ran along the outside of the home were filled with rocking chairs and families visiting with loved ones.

The daughter had been hesitant to give up the constant care of her father. But she had discovered that it was a daunting never-ending task to keep up with the increasing mood swings and disruptive behavior of a man who had always been a kind, gentle person and respected leader in the community.

As we completed what seemed to be an inordinate amount of admission papers, I noticed she looked exhausted and very close to tears. She said it had been many months since she had enjoyed a good night's sleep or had any time for her own needs.

"Dad wanders off every afternoon looking for mom and when I try to tell him she passed away some years ago, he argues with me like he doesn't even know who I am," she explained. "He seems to get real restless every evening. I can't even get him to come in and sit down with us for supper," she said with frustration in her voice.

I explained that this is called the, "Sundown Syndrome" and is something very common with Alzheimer's disease.

"We anticipate the increased anxiety and have extra staff from 4 p.m. to 9 p.m. for this reason," I said.

Part of the admission process included asking many personal questions that most family members find difficult to answer. They don't want to admit that a mom or dad who has been a loving parent, doting grandparent and independent adult now can't find the bathroom and doesn't recognize family members.

It's part of my job to coax all the information we need to provide the most appropriate care, so I gently alternate between asking intimate questions and explaining how the dementia process works.

Most of the time family members don't make the decision to find respite care, adult day care or adult foster care until all other resources have been exhausted – including themselves!

Sons and daughters have witnessed the slow decline such as missed doctor appointments, not paying bills or keeping the checkbook up to date, getting lost while driving around town, and not taking their medicines.

Family members are slow to address these needs with parents or close relatives because the reaction is usually denial and/or anger that someone is interfering in their business. Sometimes it takes a serious incident such as a car accident or kitchen fire for the family to decide that immediate action is needed. Even then, the person with early or mild stages of dementia will argue and resist any intervention.

In other situations, a spouse or child has tried to be the caregiver for too long hoping that things will get better until everyone is totally exhausted and totally out of control.

Many times I've asked a family member to go home and get some rest before trying to finish the admission paperwork.

Today Mr. Black's daughter was anxious to finish the paperwork, write me a check and get out before her dad realized what she was doing. She still feels very guilty and does not understand why her dad has changed. She offered that maybe it's his medicine or something medical that the doctors missed in his examination.

"Maybe in a few days we can take him back home, but last night he hit my husband and had a look in his eyes that I've never seen. We are really afraid he will hurt one of the kids," she said.

I made a mental note to provide 1-1 staff for the night and call the doctor in the morning for additional assessments and medication review. This was going to be a challenging case, but not unusual for our business.

Assuring her he was in good hands and walking her to the car, I told her to go home and rest and not to worry about her father tonight.

"Someone will be with him tonight and we'll take good care of your dad," I said as I gave her a hug and held the car door open. It was still very difficult for her to walk away and leave her dad standing at the window looking out - but not waving goodbye.

"'Bye Daddy", she whispered, her voice tight with pain.

Later, he had gone berserk, smashed our picture window, upset the staff and jeopardized his chances of living at our facility. It would be my job to inform the family, get the window repaired quickly and follow up on his medical care and possible re-placement.

Each day would bring different challenges, difficulties and rewards.

Yesterday it had been a heavy rainstorm that had knocked out the electric and water for a few hours. Two of the homes had water from a well that depended on electricity to provide running water. The staff had followed Teresa's severe weather precautions and filled the bathtubs with water and started a specific supper menu to be used when the power was out, but no one had anticipated that workmen on the roof had left a downspout directed straight into the basement window!

I got a call that water was running into the basement that was living quarters for the resident managers, storage for emergency supplies and the laundry room.

Not knowing the cause or what mess I would find, I rushed over and discovered the culprit downspout! Getting soaked to the skin in the process, I quickly redirected the downspout and gathered some staff to help clean up the mess.

That wasn't the first time this particular home had a severe non-medical emergency. A few months back on a blustery cold winter day, the dryer had overheated and caught the clothes on fire sending billowing clouds of black smoke upstairs to the resident living area.

At the time no one knew where the smoke was coming from but instead of calling 911 or the fire department, I had received the frantic call at home. This may have been because most of the residents actually resisted evacuation from the smoke.

As I passed the fire trucks on the way to the scene, the fire chief waved me on knowing it would take calm tact and skill to direct residents who had no fear of fire and no understanding of the instructions to gather at the front door.

I arrived in time to help evacuate the 12 elderly residents to the driveway outside as other employees and neighbors who lived nearby rushed over to help. Wrapping our own coats around their wheelchairs and grabbing blankets from beds, we had everyone in the yard fairly well "tucked in" when the first trucks arrived to check out the cause for the heavy smoke.

We were thankful for the immediate assistance and that no one suffered ill effects from the smoke. By bedtime, few of the residents even remembered the incident.

Sometimes it was a medical call in the middle of the night for someone who had fallen or was complaining of feeling sick. I would respond to examine them and determine if they needed to be sent to the hospital or if we needed to call for backup to help lift someone back into bed.

Some days I would meet the doctor as he made rounds and I would draw blood for testing or collect urine samples per his order. Everyday I monitored the pulse of the homes and made notations in the charts to keep the medical records up to date and ready for inspection on a moment's notice.

Keeping the homes at capacity was a very important responsibility that Teresa expected from me. This information was included in a weekly report I faxed to her. Already my contacts at local hospitals were set in place and at least once a week I made my rounds of all the social workers making sure they had our brochures and business cards in good supply.

At Teresa's, I actually looked forward to the state surveys. Back then, we knew that the state inspector would come armed with briefcases filled with new forms, additional forms and supplies of old forms! He would leave no stone unturned from the dark corners of the basement to the smallest chip on the kitchen counter. Teresa would challenge even the minutest deficiency and the state inspector would counter argue the slightest deviation but everyone knew that Teresa expected excellence in her homes.

Teaching families and staff about dementia was an ongoing function of my job. Even at the homes where every employee was given a constant stream of information about the devastating effects of dementia, there was always a situation that caused frustration or complicated situations that needed my professional intervention.

Every home knew that when a resident became persistently confused and agitated, they could call me for advice or assistance. Many times I would be wakened in the middle of the night to assure a resident that her cat was safe at my house or that Johnny was on his way home.

Sometimes we washed and dried the same load of washcloths and towels so a resident would feel a sense of responsibility as she folded laundry over and over again. Others helped make beds or set the table many times a day.

One stage of dementia causes a person to be so forgetful that they feel obsessed to ask the same question repeatedly. Occasionally, it was difficult to always remain calm and tolerant when we had to repeat the same answer to the same question every few seconds. Or, the answer wasn't satisfactory.

"Where is my coat?"

"It's right here."

"Oh thank you so much. Where is my coat?"

"I told you, it's right here."

"You don't have to get smart about it. Have you seen my coat?"

"See it's right here on this chair."

"Well now, how did it get there? Have you seen my coat?"

"Here put it on. It's right here."

"I'm not that dumb. Have you seen my coat?"

"This is your coat right here."

"That's not my coat. What did you do with my coat?"

By the time the staff would call me in exasperation, I'd usually have to go to the home and distract the resident by taking them to another room and redirecting the conversation to an imaginary trip to the store in their Buick Sedan. We would need to stop and get gasoline for 25 cents a gallon and pick up a loaf of bread that cost

10 cents a loaf. By the time we got "ready" for the trip, I'd have the resident in his pajamas and tucked into bed.

Forgetting one's age is common with dementia. Many of our residents didn't even think about their age but the conversation often revolved about living with mom and doing chores at home. Often a resident would become worried because a parent had not come in for the night or returned home from work before dark.

The only way to relieve those fears is to go into their reality and confront the pressing problem.

Explaining that dad had to help with a sick cow if the resident had lived on a farm; or assurance that "mama" was tending to a sick neighbor or helping birth a baby was often enough to calm an upset resident who was trying to figure out the combination to the gate and go find the missing parent.

Most family members had very little education about dementia and Alzheimer's disease. We had some very good books that we loaned out, but more often it was my duty to deal with each family in their own way and help them understand that the dementia would probably not get better; and promises that their loved one would never be put into a nursing home or left with strangers to care for them was not only unreasonable but would eventually be impossible to keep.

I encouraged family members to accept that they were not responsible for, nor could they change the course of the disease as the affected person withdrew into a private but distant world of his or her own.

Those with dementia usually don't show awareness of the disease but they do try to keep up appearances in their struggle to be their own person.

In order to help the residents keep their dignity we often slipped play money into their pocket and tried to keep everyone dressed nicely all the time.

Sometimes a good-looking older man with advanced dementia would look and act so normal at the gate that someone would comply with his request to unlock the gate, or he would just follow a visitor through the open gate and start walking down the busy highway oblivious to frantic calls for him to come back or of the fast moving traffic.

I explained that dealing with daily life becomes increasingly difficult as people suffering from dementia and Alzheimer's disease become increasingly incompetent and insecure in normal daily situations.

Sometimes, at first, the only signs of mild dementia are a facial expression that is perceived as penetrating and non-committal answers to common conversations that don't belie the lack of understanding.

"Oh, how nice" or "that's good," voiced inappropriately are subtle clues they can't hide. Pictures of food pasted to the refrigerator, pictures of a toilet on the bathroom door and pictures of clothing taped to the dresser are clues that something is not right. Keys that used to always hang on the peg are now left in the garage or even tossed into the trashcan. Cash may be hidden in the bag of cat food. The same clothing worn day after day. Notes and reminders posted all around the house. Forgetting to pay for groceries. These are all signs that must not be ignored.

One morning as I walked in the front door at one of the homes, I heard a woman screaming as if she was in terrible distress. Immediately I knew that "Betty" was getting her morning shower. We had multiple problems with Betty in this area. First of all, she denied being incontinent (wetting her pants) and we usually replaced her soiled underwear during the night with fresh clean clothing while she slept.

The second challenge was getting her into the shower or to cooperate for any washing up that included getting near water. Many of our residents had a primeval fear of water. We decided it must be the instinctive urge to survive and everyone knows that one cannot breathe in water. It is a great mystery and unique challenge that prevails in homes for the elderly anywhere.

Betty was frail and weak, so the quick warm soapy shower scream was short lived. I always dreaded coaxing strong-as-ox, but confused angry men into the shower. They didn't scream but they usually yelled obscenities and fought like angry bears in the bath. A few times the staff have been injured while trying to give a male resident a shower or bath. We found that it helped to always have at least two staff in the bathroom at bathtime. One to bathe and one to distract!

Many times I've found children having to bear the responsibility of both parents showing signs of dementia at the same time. This is the greatest burden of all times and my heart always goes out to families who have this hardship to bear.

Strong capable fathers become childlike, defiant and uncooperative. Gentle, soft-spoken mothers are confused and angry. They scream vulgar obscenities and order everyone out of the room when families try to have a discussion about current problems. They become combative with others and with each other.

The children must pull together as one to make decisions that parents would never have wanted their children to make. Family ties that are weak will break with the strain. Marriages that are not strong may fall apart. Health issues become evident and take their toll. Money woes may become a formidable mountain.

I have seen it all in the faces of our clients as I've tried to weave a strong helpline for families who have to deal with dementia, Alzheimer's, death and dying.

So, my eight years as a staff member of Teresa's Country Homes was an education I could never have obtained in a more profound way. I loved every employee, every resident and family member there. We formed a bond and friendship with each other and that will never be broken. Our impact on the community was extensive, powerful and extraordinary.

We were rewarded when comfort took the place of loss and pain. Education brought power and healing. At the end of each day, there was pride and satisfaction for a job well done.

Eventually, the business was sold to another owner and I moved to another state when life changes occurred and my goals and dreams moved forward.

*Billy plays with Brutus*

# Chapter 37

## A Reptile Hunt and Paper Routes

On April 1,1982 I sat down and wrote about a day with Billy and Philip.

**Dear Diary...**

*"My therapy has been productive and I'm viewing my world in a much more positive light now although Bill and I still have our challenging times and I sometimes wonder what's going to become of our future together. Neither of us want to cause pain or hardship for our boys."*

Waking up to a dog barking to be let outside wasn't much different in 1982 than 2005, when Sheba touches her cold nose to mine at 6:30 a.m.

Brute was Billy's medium size black dog whose best talents were digging in my flowerbed and breaking his chain.

Expecting to pull myself out of an empty bed with Bill having left hours ago for some mission at the university, I sat up and stretched my legs about to hop of our bed, but surprisingly Bill was still in bed and willing to get up and let Brute out.

It wasn't long before I heard the car leave and I sleepily wondered what had happened to that quick little good-morning and good-bye kiss.

Just then his alarm went off and my day started with a slight sadness and sudden rush to make the pre-school bus time as pleasant as possible for my boys.

Billy and Philip like several non-official calls to get up before the one that says, 'first-call", "second-call" and finally, "third call" that gets them headed for the bathroom.

No matter what time they get up, I still need to prod them each step of the process but today they are ready well ahead of time for their ride to school. Philip is playing with the black cat that is expecting kittens anytime, and Billy is roughing it with Brute who would love to chase the cat.

Now I can head for my work. My nursing job at Blossomland Learning Center is perfect for the boys' school schedule. I work at the county school for handicapped children close to our home from 8:30 a.m. until 3:30 p.m.

I've been planning some April Fool jokes for some of the staff and am successful at handcuffing the janitor to his desk and replacing Wally's coffee sugar with salt before the serious minded RN who is my boss orders me to go check the suction machines in the classrooms.

Every handicapped child knows me by name and greets me in some way as I give them their meds, tube feedings or do some treatment they need during the day. My day goes by quickly.

Arriving home after work, Philip runs to greet me with a hug. Billy is on the phone with Ed planning a "Reptile Hunt" that I agree to providing they are home by 4:30 p.m.

I have time to take a little nap on Billy's bed where the sun has been shining through the window making it cozy and warm, but the solitude lasts only about ten minutes before the phone rings.

Then it's time for a quick run to the grocery store and rounding up the boys to practice the piano for 30 minutes. This will not happen unless I coax and push them to the piano bench. While Philip is coming in to practice, I urge Billy to take Brute for a walk.

Suddenly I see black cat with a very skinny tummy! Where are her kittens? I follow her to three tiny wet kittens meowing in the basement behind the furnace. Now we have six cats, two hamsters and one dog.

I'm working at least two jobs, so tonight I'm scheduled for a short shift at the hospital. I need to clock in by 7 p.m. and it's after 5:30 already! Where did the evening go? We order Pizza and I put my hair in some quick electric rollers. Billy still hasn't taken Brute out but he is practicing his recital piece so I'll take care of Brute. should be home anytime and we will pass like ships in the night once again. I dash out the door for work as he pulls into the driveway. This time I get a "public kiss" on the sidewalk in front of the house.

Tonight I'm doing private duty for a little boy Billy's age who just had his appendix removed. He is comfortable and his mother is cautiously relaxed. That made for an unusually quiet night for me and I'm grateful for that.

Returning home about midnight, Bill is asleep. Black cat is fixed up with a kitty box, food and water and a soft nest for her kittens in Billy's room. The other cats have been banished to the back porch.

Brute is yapping at his chain and probably bothering the neighbors. The hamster cages in the living room are smelly and need to be cleaned. Bill mutters sleepily that he "forgot" to practice with Philip.

While the house is quiet I scrub the bathroom, start of load of laundry and rinse off the dishes scattered around the kitchen. A typical day in the Cash household in 1982.

# Chapter 38

## Fibs and Bibs

In December of 1984 when Billy was 14 and Philip was 9 years old, Commodore 64 Computer games were all the rage. Philip played Pitfall 11, Hero and Soccer games. Billy was into Zork. For Christmas Philip was getting a Flight Simulator and Billy's gift was Infidel.

Billy had a paper route with 35-42 customers. Both boys were taking piano lessons and practicing half an hour every day.

The boys had nicknames for each other, "Fibs" and "Bibs."

Bill and I are having some heated discussions about boarding academy for Billy. I'm vehemently opposed to sending the boys away to a boarding school such as Laurelbrook School when Andrews University has much more appropriate educational opportunities right in our back yard. We argue until Billy begs us to quit arguing about it. Neither of us are willing to compromise on our opposite points of view about this.

Four years later, Billy's 16th birthday was awful. Poor guy. It was not a good day. First of all, he woke up late and missed his bathroom time 6:15 to 6:30. Then he spilled milk all over the table and his pants. When Bill told him to clean it up, he got even more upset.

When Bill ordered him to comb his hair, he said he didn't have time.

I got out of bed to settle the commotion. I asked Billy to do something with his hair and told him he wasn't going anyplace until he did something so it wasn't sticking straight up.

Billy hit the wall with fist and said, "I hate this place. I get treated worse than dog shit. I get no respect around here!"

I told him to go into the bathroom until he could calm down (in hopes he would do something with his hair).

I almost cried when I heard him sobbing as he wet his hair. "I get treated worse than dog shit. Dog SHIT. DOG SHIT."

Just then he got a call from his friend Todd Scribner.

"Hello Todd, It's my birthday and all I get is yelled at."

Suddenly I was in tears too. If Billy only knew that I'd give anything in the world for him to be happy. I wished we didn't care how he dressed or if he ever combed his hair! If only I had the power to make his life more pleasant!

Billy slammed out the door before I could give him a hug and say Happy Birthday.

Later, Bill came back home to comfort me but I told him I could take care of myself. In a way I blamed Bill's constant nagging and counterproductive expectations of Billy and me!

At 10:30 Billy called from school to say he was sorry. I suspected that Bobby had something to do with the apology but that was appreciated too.

That evening, we offered Billy a Pizza Hut supper with five or six friends (girls and/or boys), but he opted for money ($20).

What Billy couldn't know then but perhaps does now, is that every penny I earned back then went to Bill's keeping. I was given a very small allowance and had to account for that money too. If I rented a movie from Schrader's grocery for $1.00, he took that amount from my monthly allowance of $15.00.

My last entry on Billy's birthday is looking forward to a special day for Billy in the morning. *"Tomorrow Billy goes for the written part of his driver's test."*

I hope Billy doesn't mind if I tell this story because I think many mothers and too many children have had the same kind of morning at one time or another.

The best thing we did for Billy was to take him out of the private academy and let him attend Berrien Springs High School.

Billy's teacher's there saw his talent for art and didn't rag him about his clothes and hair. He was better appreciated and began to consider college.

Sandra's son, Bobby was living with us during this time and attended high school with Billy. They got along like two peas in a pod! They got into some mischief; but we survived and they survived!

The summer of 1991, Billy was accepted at the University of Michigan. It was a bittersweet milestone for me! Billy would be 157 miles away instead of living at home and attending Andrews University, but I was relieved that he got the college of his choice and I knew that he was on a good road to success in life!

Billy took Spanish and worked with the grounds department – both areas he excelled in and felt good about. He spent his junior year in Spain and spent some time traveling abroad. I missed him but was grateful he had at last found something of his own.

On Philip's 14th birthday we took a rare family trip to Boyne Mountain skiing with Philip's friend Mark Regazzi. I didn't ski but watched from the windows as Philip went down Sugar Loaf's "Awful-Awful" three times and didn't fall.

Sometimes I wish I had let Billy and Philip guide me down the slopes until I could rush fearlessly down the long hills with the wind blowing in my face and my body flying effortlessly through the rushing cold air.

When Philip graduated from 12th grade, he spoke to his class about what he was thankful for. I cringed a little when he stepped to the podium because by then his dad and I were divorced, and he had a stepmother in his life who wasn't being very kind to him.

Philip said he remembered all the fun times he and I had going shopping. He joked about not having a "wicked stepmother" and mentioned good times with his dad. None of which I remembered like that, but I was unspeakably proud of my son that day.

I'm pleased that each boy continued his education and both became teachers.

Billy finished his masters degree in Spanish, and Philip is working on his advanced degree. Each boy talks of getting his PhD. I hope they remember the glue!

# Chapter 39

## Political Pull

If someone had told me that as young mother, I would run for an elected position, I would have been the first to laugh right out loud. Remembering my education was limited to a year of nursing and my life experience was limited to working hard every day as a nurse, I didn't realize that my experience as a newspaper reporter had impressed so many of the residents in the village and township where we lived.

The township supervisor approached me early in 1992 soon after I had resigned as the local newspaper reporter. I had covered the township meetings for several years as the local reporter. Supervisor Hildebrand said the township needed a change and he thought I would fit the bill as the Oronoko Township Clerk. He promised to support and assist with the campaign.

My kids thought it was a great idea. Bill wasn't convinced that I could win a local election. None of us had a clue of the hard work it would take for the next six months to inform the public of my interest.

A small election committee quickly formed to prepare an action plan and to get my name on the ballot. The agenda included finding additional people to form smaller committees to assure we didn't miss one point of the process in a timely manner.

I practiced my speeches, purchased suitable clothes and studied every detail of the necessary steps we had to take including filing deadlines, timelines for ordering campaign signs, wording on promotional materials and decisions for ad placements.

Mental preparation was also important. My team discussed the best way to present myself. It was important for me to believe in my success before taking the first step to convince others to support me! It would be a hard fought battle to beat a two-term township clerk who was born and raised in Berrien Springs and had vowed to not be beaten by a woman who had no political experience.

One of the most important decisions I had to make was to decide if this was going to be a nasty campaign digging up all the dirt I could get on my opponent, or just promoting my self as the most qualified person – when perhaps at the moment - I wasn't the most qualified!

From the beginning, I put the brakes on any backstabbing or negative comments in public or advertising. Some members of my committee thought this was a mistake, but I was firm. They told me this could make or break the outcome, but I didn't back down.

An invaluable amount of helpful information and guidance came from an unexpected source. Fred Cash, Bill's younger brother, had spent many years working with campaign committees in California. He kept in touch and encouraged me with a long list of good ideas I used to increase my chances of winning.

My mind boggled with all the information coming in! After filing the paperwork by the mandatory deadline and determining that I would run as a Republican, we assigned responsibilities. Then we assigned people to monitor the assignments!

First, we needed a list of all the registered voters who could vote for me. That list of about 4,000 voters was purchased from the county local clerk's office. We divided the list into smaller sections for several teams to use throughout the campaign.

Every prospective voter would be contacted in various ways more than once during the next several months and again as the primary election drew near. They would be encouraged to vote for Linda Cash, Township Clerk!

Most people do not realize that when two people are running for the same position in the same party, the Primary Election determines whose name will be on the November ballot. If my supporters didn't vote for me in the earlier Primary Election, I had no chance of winning!

That was our first challenge. Get support for the August Primary!

We used the name Cash in various ways as ticklers to help people get used to the name they would see on the ballot. We made up green paper flyers the size of dollar bills with the name Cash on both sides. It included information about me and the most important date – Primary Election Day.

These unusual flyers were scattered all over town in grocery bags, placed on doorknobs, handed out by members of the committee and in mass mailings. People were encouraged to keep one in their wallets, purses and posted on refrigerators. It wasn't long before my little green flyers were blowing through the air on windy days or tucked into unexpected nooks and crannies in every home.

Signs were placed on every street corner in the yards of friends and neighbors. We had to obtain permission for every sign we planted in the ground! We went the extra step to created large 4x8 billboards "Vote for Linda Cash" and planted these signs at each entrance of the town.

We encouraged letters to the editor from family, co-workers and friends. We decided what I would say in interviews for the papers.

I bought a couple of red outfits to wear when going door to door and walking in parades or to the fireman's pancake breakfast. I spoke at the Optimist Club and other events throughout the summer.

To boost my confidence, I had to feel the energy and belief in myself. One committee was established just to keep tabs on my energy level and encourage me along the way. I practiced my speeches to the dog, the kitchen stove, the bedroom mirror and anyone who would listen. I read motivational and inspirational books and kept post-it's all around the house and in the car telling myself what a great person I was! I had to believe it to preach it!

The supervisor who had many years' experience as a township official and had a large following, drove me to the homes of his supporters and introduced me to his friends and neighbors.

My entire campaign team spent many evenings walking door to door with my flyers and campaign material. We didn't let summer storms slow us down. We didn't take vacations. We put band-aids on the numerous blisters on our feet and kept moving every day promoting the campaign and my name.

We checked off each section of town that I personally covered door-to-door and to our knowledge, I made it to every door in the village of almost 2,000 residents.

On the date of the Primary Election, (not in November as many still believed), we followed Fred's advice and added a new, "Vote Today" message to the top corner of every sign we had posted around town. Each team called every name on their portion of the registered voter list and reminded them to vote. The prepared message was the same for everyone and included the proper place for each person to vote and the time that the polls closed that night.

We had a special team in place to transport those who needed a ride to the polls. I made myself visible at each polling precinct, but not illegally so.

Still, on election night, I had the jitters as we gathered in the hotel suite we had reserved for the celebration that everyone assured me would end positively.

We nibbled on treats and listened to the radio reports of election results. There was also a big battle going on with the sheriff department that we hoped would win a victory for that incumbent too.

Just after news reports declared our favorite sheriff as the winner, I answered the phone to hear my opponent's voice on the line. She was congratulating me on winning the election. She would be the first to know who won because it was her job to report the results of the election to the county clerk and news outlets. She recorded her own loss and called to congratulate me!

I was about to step in to a new arena of my life. One that required well-fitting shoes, a hard hat and tough skin!

My greatest strength came from well qualified, experienced office employees and managers who knew the ropes of the clerk's position, and kept me walking the fine line of keeping promises made and working together with the township team.

Taking minutes of the board meeting was vastly different but somewhat related to covering the meetings for the newspaper as a reporter. As clerk, I attended training sessions to learn the process for setting up polling booths on each Election Day to assure that every step of each election went smoothly and in accordance with the laws.

My staff kept the registered voter cards standing at attention in massive files at the township hall. Sometimes it took courage to have the only "nay" vote at board meetings on subjects that conflicted with my campaign promises regarding new rental ordinances and a proposed water and sewer system for the township. The township was also developing a new municipal building that required a lot of planning.

I was an excellent township clerk, but I hated the politics. My negative votes were not always popular with the board. In 1996 I ran again for township clerk and won a second term, but by then I had learned that politics is not what you see in public, but what goes on behind closed doors. It's not what political officials say in meetings but how they vote in the end. I had discovered that politics is governed by the unwritten rules.

Soon after my second term ended and I was out of politics, the voters organized a recall election that eliminated the position of everyone on the township board except the supervisor and treasurer. That's politics.

# Chapter 40

## *I Want Off at The Next Stop*

**B**illy and Philip are the most blessed part of my entire life. While I cannot write about or even mention the names of all the people who have been a rich part of my life experience; the past, present and future rests in my children and my love and admiration for each of my boys.

Now that I'm looking forward to being a grandmother, I recall so many moments in the past when I could have been a better mother.

Yes, once when they were very small (long before running for township clerk), I jumped off the Cash Express for a while because life seemed hopeless. I felt useless and in the way. It seemed my life was nothing but a bother to the family. The train was going too fast and I couldn't keep up! I honestly thought no one would care or even miss me. I didn't feel worthy to be the mother of such sweet boys.

I don't talk about it today. I wonder if my boys remember those brief moments in time when I wasn't strong and sure of myself. I felt beaten down, unloved, unwanted and unappreciated. I couldn't remember the last time anyone in my family had said the words, "I love you."

Billy was seven years old and had just finished 6-year old kindergarten. Every day it was harder and harder for me to get out of bed and face the day. For one thing, my joints hurt so badly that I couldn't get dressed by myself. My elbows often felt like someone had put a hot nail into each joint and the pain got worse every time I moved my arms. My stomach hurt all the time – like a hot knife from between my shoulder blades through to my stomach. My hips hurt with a throbbing pain all the way to my ankles. I couldn't lie down on either side without feeling like I was lying on a boil.

Then there was the feeling that I was worthless. I felt like the Cash family was a tribe of Indians that I did not belong to. (I wrote that in my diary.) I couldn't remember the last time Bill told me I had done a good job at anything. It seemed that everything I did wasn't quite good enough or not done the way he would have done it. I felt like his parents thought I wasn't a good mother but, for the life of me, I couldn't figure out what they wanted me to do differently.

Eventually, I was certain that everyone would be happier if I were out of the picture. Then things could be done just they way they wanted it. People wouldn't be frustrated. The boys would be happy with their dad because he did all the fun things with them anyway while I was always working.

Bill would be able to do as he pleased, and I wouldn't be a handicap for his lifestyle. Maybe if I weren't around, Bill would enjoy his work and be happier when he was at home. He surely didn't seem happy with me in the picture.

I wrote in my diary, *"I feel so left out and alone."*

I now realize how off base I was in my thinking, but my world seemed to be breaking apart and I couldn't hang on any longer. I believe I left a note saying goodbye and I hope it said, I love you, because I always loved my babies.

I left on a Greyhound bus for parts unknown. I honestly thought that everyone would be glad to have me out of the picture. I did not feel loved or appreciated anymore.

At that time, they didn't have Amber Alert, but I'm not sure my husband would have called the troops to look for me. He found church friends to look after Billy and Philip, and his parents were living close by to provide prayers and support.

I honestly cannot remember how long I was gone. I went to grandma's and she sent me back to Missouri with old friends. (Still a place to hide from the world!) It seems like I was there only a few days before I was in an accident and hospitalized. I had a few quiet days in the hospital to worry and think about my life. No one rushed to my side and I wondered if I would be welcome when I returned or cast aside as more trouble than I was worth! When I got released from the hospital, I flew back home in shame and bewilderment.

Surprisingly, when I returned, Bill's mother was my biggest supporter. Bill couldn't understand the true reason for my worthless feelings, and complained about the money we had to put on the credit card to fly me back home!

It was time for me to get some professional help to understand my feelings and work through them in a positive way.

**I needed to learn how to be the conductor, the brakeman and the engineer!**

We had gone into parenthood without training or experience. I had no parents of my own to set an example, no classes on parenting, no mentors to follow and not even good friends to talk to. It happens one day and you are holding a tiny baby in your arms. This is life! For me, this was love!

When Billy was born, his dad brought a basketball to the hospital. ~~Everything his dad had and had not succeeded in, I believe he thought Billy would do.~~ Have the best education. Be great in sports and become an avid sports fan. Be smart, popular and fashionable. Become a good law abiding citizen. President of his class. President of the United States! We spoke about all that when Billy was born.

It was a bit much to expect from Billy. I saw the challenges ahead for my first-born son and wished I could make life easier for him, but his dad made my life just as exacting, and I wasn't made to be like that either. I didn't have the knowledge or insight to change back then.

Billy was always original. He had his own baby talk and a vivid imagination. His imaginary friend, Maynard, ate the food Billy didn't like or hid toys he couldn't find. When Billy was about four years old, he said Maynard had gone to live with one of his friends for a few days, but Maynard resurfaced again when Billy was a teenager.

He was sure of himself and he became a loving big brother to baby Philip. Later, I was glad to see Billy enjoy ski trips and baseball games with his dad. There were times when I thought my teenage son might prefer to live under a bridge rather than at home. I knew that when he was free to spread his wings, he would find himself and be happy!

Hopefully the civilization Bill and I created will cultivate a better understanding of relationships and how to make them work.

196

Maybe I wasn't ready to be a parent. Maybe I didn't play with them enough. Maybe I was gone to work too much. Maybe I didn't provide a sparkling home and the finest meals. Maybe I argued with their dad too often. Maybe I wasn't there when they really needed me.

Did I hug them enough? Did I instill truth and honesty? How many times did I tell them how proud I was of them? Did I show unconditional love? Have I helped them spread their wings and fly? Was my love enough to connect with my children for a lifetime?

Sometimes I ask myself these questions because I know I was unprepared to be a parent. Whatever I did right was pure gut instinct and intuition. Billy and Philip are smart and loving and forgiving. They don't have children yet, but if they ever do, I'm sure they will recognize the parental feelings of pride and joy that I feel for them.

Today, we don't live near enough to visit more than a few times a year. But we appreciate cell phones, e-mail and modern technology for communication. Billy and Katy live in Oregon. Philip and Shelly live in Michigan. Every time we talk, I feel their love, devotion and strength – and we always say, "I love you!" Unlike many families, our times together are always magical and happy. People tell me that I must have done something good to have such fine boys!

*Philip (left) and Billy Cash*

# Chapter 41

## *Help Wanted – Inquire Within*

As a young mother and wife, I knew that I had to do something about the insecurity I felt about myself – and soon! My conditioned "yes" response was killing me. Most every time I wrote in my diary, I ended with two helpless options. Dying or running away. And running away hadn't helped!

I felt like a giant sponge that was saturated with everybody's problems. I was a leader in the community and at church, but trusted no one with my inner struggle to feel accepted and appreciated.

Bill and his parents finally agreed that something was wrong, and we all agreed that it was "me" that needed to be "fixed." I wanted to be a good mother, loving wife and be able to make Bill happy.

A peek into my diaries over the next several years of therapy doesn't reveal any deep dark secrets. My visits with Dr. Berecz began with what seemed like days and days of nothing but tears. I cried and cried and cried and he handed me tissues and tissues and more tissues.

It was the first time in my life I had someone to talk to who was not critical, not complaining, not asking and not condemning. He made it clear that he wanted nothing from me, and we would talk when I felt like talking.

Over time, his gentle prodding questions resulted in simple answers that seemed like talking to myself. He wasn't going to take advantage of my weakness. He wasn't going to try to change me into someone I didn't know.

We discussed what a three-year old child feels like when they are abandoned, and I was surprised to realize that a child is

...ced they have done something wrong. We reviewed my caretaking compulsion that started in childhood and was reinforced by grandma's unrealistic demands, and why this pattern was not healthy for my family or me.

When I tried to convince him I wasn't as "smart" as Bill, he gave me an IQ test that showed I was. When I told him I didn't hate grandma or my mother, he told me it was okay to be angry at what they had done to me. To my surprise, I discovered that I was allowed to have an opinion and that I was very capable of making my own decisions!

When he learned that I'd never been to a movie or to a restaurant alone, we planned how I would go out to eat by myself and appreciate being waited on. Later, an assignment included attending a movie alone and ignoring grandma's persistent voice telling me how much of a sinner I was, or Bill's warning in my ears about the money it cost!

We slowly walked the paths of my childhood, teenage and young adults years. Somehow he knew I had a strength within that needed a gentle nudging to the sun. His work was to guide my mind to open the doors I had closed, and for me not to fear what I might find. Instead of locked doors, dark rooms and finger-pointing ghosts, I found golden nuggets of boldness, intelligence, courage, strength and peace.

Alas, Bill chose not to open those doors with me. He was too far ahead of me on his life's journey to reach back and take my hand. _He truely tride but the Chasm was_

Today, new nuggets appear when I least expect them! Heart stopping nightmares are rare now, and past fears are less intense. The conditioned responses will always haunt me, I'm sure, but anytime I start to feel insecure and frozen with fear, I remember white tissues at the end of those fingertips of one who answered the cry for, "Help Wanted!" He said, "Look Within."

_Too great._

# Chapter 42

## Diaries Argue the 'D' Word
### (Diary Reflections 1985 – 1991)

**November 2, 1985**
**Dear Diary....**

"*I*'*m troubled today and I hope by spitting this out in my diary, I'll feel better.*

*I seem to have a split problem. Bill and myself. It seems I never win! God knows I've tried to adjust to Bill and this hectic life we live. Bill told me last night, 'We haven't gotten any closer to understanding each other in 15 years.'*

*I feel confused, empty, sad, depressed, lonely, angry, frightened and panicky. What's going to happen with my life?*

*I think Bill is a thread's distance from walking out. He threatens to at any moment. It's not the fact that Bill might leave that's so frightening. I think I could really handle that and face the fire, but it's him holding that over my head all the time.*

*And it's the kids having to deal with it and me having to deal with the kids and me having to deal with me! For what have I done?*

*It's hard not to feel worthless. Everything I think I have accomplished in my marriage, Bill seems to think I have not. Am I a good wife? He says I am. He says he doesn't understand my outbursts of anger or periods of depression even though when I feel this way, I repeatedly reassure him by saying, 'Honey, it's not you.'*

*I try to open my heart to him and tell him what's bothering me and you know what he does then? He starts telling me about all his problems.*

He says we don't have any close friends. 'Not one. Because you don't like to socialize.' Storming around the bedroom where we try to keep out voice down, he says, 'I can never do what I want. I always have to sacrifice for you.'

It turns my heart cold. I would disappear forever if I could think of a way without hurting my boys. They don't want us to argue and beg us to stop.

Last night Bill said he had three options. 'Get out. Shut-up or get help'

Well, after all that Bill couldn't think of any more reasons why he was unhappy with me. When I suggested we talk about the problems he had just brought up, he said I had misunderstood everything he had just said.

'You're the best wife I could ever have,' he says. 'It's me that needs help. I'm very frustrated and unhappy with myself. You poor thing. What I have put you through!'

I suggested that maybe he should leave the kids and me. 'Make it an option and not a possibility,' I argued.

His unhappy response was, 'Oh, so you want to get rid of me!'

I replied that if he actually left, he might realize what he really had. I also added that I might not let him come back.

'He's so selfish,' I wrote in my diary. Oh well, maybe he's not. Maybe I am. I guess neither of us should leave each other. 'I'd just like to die."

## August 29, 1986
## Dear Diary....

"Boy, am I down. I feel like nobody loves me even though I know they do – or do they? Everything seems so heavy. Even the pesky fly on my hand! I feel like everybody uses me for all I have to give and then discards me when they're done.

I was awake all night listening to a drug raid at the trailer park, expecting a call for the correspondent to take pictures. That should be my call. I usually run at the first fire tone on the scanner, but I know they don't want pictures of undercover officers at a drug raid, so I wait half-awake waiting for the phone to ring. But dispatch calls another correspondent from out of the area. Must be a new dispatcher.

Then I jump up for a house fire at 3 a.m. and stay at the scene

202

*until we know there are no injuries. This morning the editor tells me that my film from the fire didn't come out. One of the few times in five years as the newspaper correspondent for our town that the f-stops are set wrong on my camera! The newspaper probably wouldn't use the pictures anyway because no one was killed!*

*Sandra's teenage son Bobby is living with us now. Sandra doesn't have any way to support him and his father who is a cardiologist doesn't want to make time for him. I enrolled Bobby in school yesterday. Then last night Bobby's father calls and says to send Bobby back to Detroit with him. Now I have to drop Bobby from school, go collect the deposit, get Bobby packed and make reservations for a trip neither of us want him to take!*

*I've decided to quit my five-year job at Lee Memorial Hospital and go into private duty work. Today I give my months' notice. I sure hope this will work out!*

*Bill is never home. Never comes to bed with me. Never makes a decision. It's either his dissertation or his second job in Niles which is money I never see and we're always still in the hole. My kids are growing up so fast! Computer games. Friends over. Paper route. Homework. Piano practice. Computer games. Friends over. Paper route. Homework. Piano practice. ..."*

## December 7, 1986
## Dear Diary...

*"Well, it's four months later. I sent Bobby to Detroit and his father sent him back! Guess things weren't convenient enough for his dad. Robert had to get up at 5:45 a.m. to take Bobby to catch his ride for school. I love him and worry that my family will destroy his sweetness and sensitivity. But at the age of 15, if that hasn't been destroyed yet, nothing will. I feel like Super Mom. Super Wife. Super Granddaughter. Super Newspaper Reporter. Super Nurse. Super Friend. Super Aunt.*

*Billy and Bill still can't get on the same wavelength. He puts so much energy into being a good father, but he can't keep it together on the little things where it really counts!*

*If we ever get a divorce, it will be over the little things. They just keep chipping away at my heart!*

*Like yesterday morning. I let Bobby stay home because he*

had a sore throat. Bill says, 'He was fine yesterday. Did you take his temperature? Does he have a fever?'

'No, I don't know if he has a fever! Would you have taken his temperature or just sent him off to school because it was the right thing to do?'

I yell at Bill. 'I worked as a nurse all weekend. I hurt. I'm tired. My knees won't move without cracking. My hands are swollen and hurt. My stomach hurts like someone stuck a hot knife in it. Philip's alarm didn't go off and he's upset. He can't find any clean socks because nobody dried the clothes last night. Muffy peed on the carpet again. Dishes are piled in the sink. There's no milk in the house for breakfast and no bread to make lunches! And you want to complain because I let Bobby stay home?'

Philip has a class at 7 a.m. but Bill says he can't take him to school because he has a meeting with his boss at the college this morning about his position there. They might cut his job. Just like that. That's the first I've heard that Bill's job was in jeopardy. That's how much we talk these days."

## December 7, 1987
## Dear Diary...

"How ironic. It's been exactly one year to the day that I open this diary again.

I'm still not on the same wavelength with Bill. We can't agree on much of anything that matters. I want to let Billy go to Pebblewood for concerts in Bridgman but he doesn't. Yet, he allows Billy and Bobby to go to Rock Concerts in Chicago. Maybe he's glad to get them out of the house for the night. I want to go to church and he's always tired. I want him to get a better paying jog, but he doesn't want to leave church work. I think his secretary gets more information than I do. I try so hard to please Bill so he will be happy. My friends say I'm not myself when I'm with him. How warped is that?"

## July 10, 1988
## Dear Diary...

"Here I am again. It's 18 months later and I'm angry with Bill again. Every time I open my diary and read what I wrote the last time, it's always the same. I wonder if Bill is just as frustrated and utterly angry with me too? And we both think we try so hard!

I quit my hospital job last month. (Kept putting it off, didn't I?) I almost forgot to tell Bill before the end of the month's notice. I feel like he wouldn't care anyway. Maybe he feels the same way about me. Neither of us have the courage to take the bull by the horns and broach the subject.

Lee Memorial was such a nice place to work. It was 20 miles away so I had time to relax and let go of family stuff before I got there. The supervisors were nice. My co-workers were friendly and such good friends. I was making $8.83/hour and had just gotten my five-year pin.

I told myself that I'd start the RN course at Lake Michigan College this year but realized that wouldn't happen. Today I decided, 'not yet.' There are too many problems when I'm away from home. Bill calls me at work every hour or so. In fact, my last evaluation at work listed my only problem was getting too many calls from home.

'Billy and Bobby are skateboarding in front of the village hall again.' 'I can't find my last Time Magazine.' 'Muffy won't go outside for me!' ' Grandma wants you to bring her peanut butter and eggs in the morning.'

Why did I quit? Maybe because it hurt so badly. How crazy is that?

No, I need to give everything I can to keeping my family together. Bill will continue to work on his PhD. I will probably always be a great LPN and hope my children realize someday that I was there for them the best that I could."

**May 8, 1989**
**Dear Diary...**

"Well, It's almost a year later and I think we're still mad at each other most of the time. I feel like if I could just do one thing exceptionally well, if we had enough money to pay all the bills, if I could devote every moment of my life catering to Bill's every want, or if Bill's favorite sports team always won, we could be a happy couple. It's such a struggle for me to try or wish for that to happen and I feel like a failure because I cannot make him happy.

In March, I officially started my photography business called, Magic Moments Photography. Bill said I could do this if I still bring in income from nursing.

Now I have a studio in the basement and specialize in wedding photography. It means everybody has to answer the business phone properly and the kids have to be in 'business mode' if I have customers at the house. No one can ask, 'When are we going to eat?' if I'm taking pictures in the studio.

Also, Bill's dad is out of the country for several months and asked me to pay his bills and keep an eye on his place. 'Don't make any special trips to the farm,' he says. But the renter doesn't pay the rent, and the electricity will be turned off tomorrow if I don't take care of both things.

Grandma is waiting for groceries and a trip to the doctor. I must make the doctor appointment at a time when I can take her. I run her to St. Joseph for her $10 food stamps and go get her meds every month. Phil is playing soccer and I should be there. Billy is working at Twixwood Nursery and needs a ride back and forth most of the time. Bobby needs transportation to Niles for his work there.

I'm still working almost every day doing private duty for several agencies. (At least I don't get written up for taking too many calls from home.)

Bill was offered the position of Director of Institutional Research at St. Mary's College at Notre Dame. Do you know what that means? It means a GIANT increase in pay and benefits. It means he will have a secure job and we might not have to see each other so much. But, he says he will turn it down because he wants to go on an archeological dig in Jordan this summer through Andrews University and he can't go if he quits that job.

Our finances are so awful that he wouldn't pay me my $57 in personal money I had coming this month because he paid for a nursing book I ordered that cost $57.23. When I argued about the money he says, 'I think I'll just move out. Everybody wants money and I don't have it!'

He complains that he is in a 'lose-lose' situation with work. He complains because I (Linda) have to work so hard and because Philip hasn't started his homework and we'll be up until midnight. He says he doesn't have money to fix the front door or the downstairs shower. He hasn't paid half the bills for April and there just isn't any 'clear cut answer' to anything.

I responded that my 'clear cut answer' for everything is a nice hot bath that I am running the water for right now. He doesn't see any humor in that and storms out to a school board meeting in Eau Claire.

I take my hot bath, shave my legs, talk to Muffy and listen to the radio while I write. Philip has no problem with his homework. It's actually nice to be home alone.

But I don't know if Bill and I are going to ever be able to have a quiet, loving, equal conversation. Our trains are going in opposite directions at out-of-control speeds."

## March 9, 1991
## Dear Diary...

"Today is our 20<sup>th</sup> wedding anniversary. Nothing special is planned It's almost two years since my last entry. I'm almost 41 years old and just discovered I can't read the letters on my diary lock. I'm showing signs of getting old. My eyes are changing. My hair is turning gray. My joints hurt like a very old woman. My fingers swell with edema. I'm on asthma medicine and I have migraine headaches most every day.

I think we both dread our anniversary every year because of the intimacy that's expected. I was scheduled to work two jobs for 16 hours today before I remembered what day it was. The agency let me off from both assignments.

After dinner at Bill's favorite restaurant, the Olive Garden, and going to see the movie, 'Greencard' and he proclaimed it, 'the best anniversary ever.'

Each day we are like ships passing in the night. We do more for and with our boys than with each other. Our energy is spent before we meet, and our 'good times' take all our strength.

This year Billy goes off to college. I can't imagine having a son that old. Where has my life gone? I'll miss my oldest child. I felt like he needed me here more than anyone else. I had a special purpose to try and help make his path smoother between him and his dad. There will be one less reason for me to be here.

*Bill and I go to great extremes to avoid having to be alone together. But then there are a moments when we get along so well that I think to myself, 'Maybe I've got it all wrong?'*

*I've always maintained to those who would offer marriage advice, 'No one knows what goes on behind closed doors. So please don't be our judge and advocate.'*

*Because we have the ability to hide the pain. Because we are smart enough to fool the world – or because the world is smart enough to look the other way – we continue in our private hells.*

*Are we sacrificing our souls to continue this facade of a marriage?*

*Will either of us ever be able to unlock the shackles that hold us together? Will either of us ever have the courage to say, 'We are doing each other more harm than good.'*

*Or will we continue slowly dying in ourselves until we don't see the rainbows, the flowers or finally, the sunshine that creates the shadows of our lives?"*

# Chapter 43

## *Siblings Reunite in New York City*

A s my long lost brother, Thomas, flew into my sister's arms and camera flashes lit the airport terminal in New York City, I knew in that moment that 35 years of searching for my mother and siblings were worth every frustrating minute!

I held in my hands a heavy briefcase full of family history that I had collected over two generations. I had been to most every capital city on the Eastern coast, written dozens of letters and made hundreds of phone calls over the years. I knew more about my family then they knew about themselves.

In 1990, I finally located our two siblings who were separated from us when our mother disappeared. We still hadn't unearthed any information about our mother, but I had located Allison and Thomas. In the process, I had also discovered our mother's sister and other relatives living within a few miles of where we had been together four decades ago! My diary is kind enough to refresh my memory of the smallest details during my first visit to see my lost siblings and other relatives in New York.

Especially touching are the faded memories of our family reunion held in June 1990. So much happened in just a few days that only the recorded moments in time and the newspaper accounts can piece together the bittersweet picture.

My brother Thomas was nine years old and my older sister Allison was a little seven-year-old child the last time we were together. Now we are all middle aged and married, divorced, getting divorced or soon-to-be widowed! Allison is a RN and Thomas is a police officer.

Would the thrill of our reunion last? Would this family be able to look beyond mistakes of the past and remake a future together? Could we mesh our personalities and life experiences into the civilization of a new family? The odds are against us.

There are too many silent heartaches behind the smiling faces and too many family secrets that have been let out of the box. Are we prepared to trust these strangers now called our brothers and sisters?

And, where in this world is our mother? Dorothyann Silver, Cleveland, Brantley, Harrison, Bowden, Phillips. Born December 12, 1928. According to our mom's sister, she may have had any of these last names. How does she know this? I ask, but her lips are sealed.

The reunion is exciting but heartbreaking at times. There are tender moments, shocking events and traumatic reactions. We have tearful arguments and comforting words. The trip is nerve-racking but rewarding.

I record on July 2, 1990, *"This trip is like heaven and hell."*

Four months earlier, I had first located Thomas's house after calling the New York area code for Thomas Cleveland as I had done for the last 20-plus years.

His mother-in-law recognized my story of four children being abandoned in NYC as it related to Thomas. He was one of those four children. But she told me that he was out of town so I would have to call back in a few days.

Unable to wait, I called her back and asked for any information about Allison or the rest of the family. She gave me our mother's sister's phone number on Staten Island.

Knowing I was very close to finding the truth scared me to death. I practiced how I would make that call to Edna (our mom's sister) with a professional people-finder, John Heide, who was assisting me with the search.

That call started a chain-reaction of calls to inform my siblings that things were not like they had been raised to believe and they had two sisters looking for them.

So, today is another magical July 4 in my life!

I'm sitting on the front porch at Thomas's house in upstate New York – everyone calls him "TJ" but he doesn't like that name.

It's 6 a.m. and as I write in my diary before t
up, the birds are flying all around me. I think I have b
but hopefully the bottle of cough medicine will ea
cough.

Thomas and I have gotten closer a little faster than with the
others. But not too close. We will see what today brings. I still feel
strange in all this.

Thomas said he can tell I'm not happy. What a statement to
one who thinks she always shows a happy face!

*No doubt there is an inner loneliness that those who've been
there recognize when they see it!* He says sometimes he's happy and
sometimes he's not. At least he is honest.

When I'm asked if I'm happy, I honestly don't know how
to answer. I know finding Dorothy is not going to be the answer.
Coming here has not been the answer either.

Allison is thrilled that we have found each other. She and her
long-time partner, Tom, have opened their home to us and organized
many excursion trips back to the city of our birth.

Our mom's sister (Edna) is cautious and slow to explain much
about what happened to our mother. She and Allison have screamed
at each other and gotten it out of their system for now. Aunt Edna
says she has pictures of all of us together as babies that she will show
us "some day".

She is still bitter toward our mother and gives vague hints
about where she might be and what her current last name is. How
does she know this much? Has she been in contact with our mother
these 40 years? Does that mean she is alive?

Edna and Thomas (TJ) are quite close and committed. He
gives her credit for raising him when no one else was there.

I'm sure by now that Edna's attitude and possible specific
actions had some relationship to our mother's leaving, but I'm wise
enough to leave it alone for now.

I think of how things are topsy-turvy back at home with my
horribly busy schedule and wish I could make more time for my
boys and myself. I don't want them growing up not knowing their
mother!

211

It's about 7 a.m. now and the bird sounds are changing. I hear a shrill bird's "whip-poor-will" like the one heard so many years ago on early Missouri mornings!

Later, Thomas and I will attend the July 4 parade in his town. I was supposed to be on Staten Island today but decided to return by train in the morning and spend one more day with Thomas.

Sandra got really upset at me for my change of plans and said some angry words, but I have been chastised by her before and know the ugliness won't last.

Thomas chews me out for crying when Sandra fusses at me. Sandra has accused me of being, "too uptight and no fun to be around."

I feel like I should get more credit for getting this family together. Instead I feel responsible for the fighting. It's not my fault everyone isn't getting along perfectly. Or is it?

It's difficult to explain to Thomas why I'm so hurt. I just cry and can't stop crying.

He says with his police officer superiority, *"Go ahead, feel sorry for yourself and jump off a bridge while you're at it."*

Then he takes my face into his hands and says, *"You can take what she says any way you choose. But it takes practice to be able to hand it right back and smile."*

At the parade, Thomas knows everyone by name! From the kids in the baseball league to the pretty lady commissioner to his good friend Bill who leads a marching band with a funny swing to his hips. Bill's completely bald head is sunburned and his white tee shirt almost hides the pager he would use in case of a real emergency!

Thomas laughs and claps and waves to everybody! He gives directions to people and smiles and greets his two girls and ex-wife sitting down in front of McDonalds. He gives a little flag to a mentally disabled man and buys ice cream for everyone around.

Later we take a little walk in the woods by Tom's house. Tom watches me stomp around while he sips his gin. I wear his cut-offs that fit perfectly.

It's terribly hot but he won't take off his shirt. "Not in front of a lady." And I won't take off my bra even though it's what the women around here do when it's hot!

When Tom is impressed with something he says," Praise the Lord." His nice home is a reflection of many years of hard work but it is mostly silent now. He is divorced and his two grown daughters are on their own.

Soon I will leave this peacefulness and tranquility, but will take with me the memory of a kindhearted brother who must fight his demons alone.

As he says good-bye at the train station, my last mental picture of Thomas is his serious but smiling face at the window of the train. *"Keep smiling,"* he says through the glass.

The 2½-hour train ride runs along a sparkling river all the way, but I'm too tired to take pictures. The ticket cost $8.75, plus Thomas gave me $20. I have 10 rolls of film that I will take home to remember the new family faces and the sights of this long awaited trip.

Back in New York City I make a list of things I didn't want to ever forget.

This list is rewritten just as it is recorded in my diary.

1. The Staten Island Ferry. (Back then it cost 25 cents to ride one way.) One day when our new family was in a muck, Allison took me to the ferry and I rode back and forth for three hours! Regardless of public opinion, I could ride the ferry every day and not get tired of it. I suggest that it could quite easily be renamed the, "Lake Michigan Linda Express."

2. The Colgate Clock. I rate it as a #1 landmark!

3. The huge glass windowed building in downtown NYC. I have several pictures of it with reflections of the sky and other buildings in it. I would like to see this building replanted in Berrien Springs!

4. The NYC skyline is always different depending on the angle, but I love it best from the ferry side. The two tall "Twin Towers" and the Empire State Building

right behind it. From the New Jersey angle, the ESB is miles away.

5.   The ferry train that rumbled over Allison's kitchen every few minutes. One gets used to the quiet rumble.

6.   I enjoyed watching the homeless people…everywhere. They aren't actually homeless; they just don't live in a house. They are quite protective of their territory whether it is on an island in the center of Broadway Street, behind a bench at the ferry, the dark corners of the subway or under a bridge.

7.   The large sea vessels on the Hudson River were awesome. Especially at night when twinkling lights mixed with lights of all types everywhere else. At night the city lights dance around and the harbor lights glow steady. The stars are forever near - as they have always been to watch over (us).

8.   I met many people in a pleasant fleeting way. The shoeshine man on the ferry who shined my shoes (and practically ruined them) for $1.75. His name is Bowan. The Captain came by and put his hat on my head and took my picture.

9.   Also, the good-natured truck driver I stopped in traffic so Allison could take a picture of NYC. I looked up at him and said, "Thank-you. I'm from Michigan." He laughed and waved good-by.

10.  There was the lawyer on the elevator who stepped out to let us off, held the door and then got back on.

11.  The tired cook on the ferry at 10 p.m. who had to return to work at 4 a.m. His parakeets were waiting

at home. He said he needed to water them and he hoped they hadn't gotten too hot during the day.

12. The couple on the ferry I took a long tele shot of. They kept their eyes on each other and their faces close. Maybe honeymooners. I could feel the love.

13. The crazy-acting black boy on the ferry running back on forth yelling, "I just need one more drink!"

14. The Downs Syndrome kids on a tour to see the Stature of Liberty from the deck of the ferry. They were very happy and swinging their hips to the movement of the ferry.

15. The beer delivery guy who, when I asked directions to where Aunt Edna works on Wall Street, (Yes the Stock Exchange is there), pointed out the directions then showed me a shortcut. "It's a long way," he advised.

16. Meeting Uncle Buddy (mom's brother) at his office and listening to him try to introduce us. First he said Allison was his sister and I was his niece. Then both of us were his nieces. Finally, he said, "They're mine!"

17. My private visit with Judy, Thomas's ex-wife. We had a wonderful exchange for about an hour. She thanked me for caring about "Tom" and advised me to take care of myself "first."

# The Answer To Her Sorrow

My mother went away when I was but a child.
She had promised to return – and I waited for a while.
Then I started looking, the search took 40 years
Of watching skies for planes, ringing phones and fears
That I wasn't any closer to the one I held so dear!
I finally found my sister Allison and older brother Tom
After all those years! That was quite a bomb!
We held a great reunion. Our memories old and dim.
But the mystery of our mother, looked as ever grim.
Could it be that we would never find
The one we one who gave us birth?
Did she really go away expecting to return?
Or, would her memory always be
A fleeting ghost that burns?
I wrote one last poem. I had to say goodbye.
She's traveling down a lonesome road and to others does not tell
Of what she's had to take in stride, the solitary hell.
Yesterday we found our mother and four more siblings too!
Somehow they knew our mother's heartache.
The clues so very few.
She had faced each tomorrow with hope that she would find
The answer to her sorrow.  The little children left behind.

~Linda Cash 2/12/1990

*36 years almost to the day that my mother wrote the good-bye letter, I found her in the same town of the letter's postmark! I had searched records in that area for the wrong last name.*

# Chapter 44

## The Pivotal Moment!

We're finally on our way! It's the reunion that almost didn't happen. The family that nearly lost each other forever. I had almost given up. I had written the last poem. Made the last entry in my journal. Accepted the advice of others that it might be just as well to quit searching for my mother.

Suddenly, one last call to the east coast and the man on the phone is telling me that our mother is alive and well in Waterbury, Connecticut! My search had come to an abrupt end when I placed "one more" inquiry call to Naugatuck, Connecticut looking for a woman with the last name of Bowden – a name suggested by our mom's sister who said she had not heard from our mother since she left.

When I explained that I was searching for a woman who had lost four children in New York City, Rick interrupted me to say he was my brother and mom lived just down the street!

I argued, "I'm not looking for a brother. I'm looking for my mother."

"I know. I'm your brother. We have the same mother," he replied with confidence!

Yes, he was right! The search had taken so long that I couldn't believe it had ended so simply! I had three more brothers and one sister I had never met!

Two days later Bill and I were making the 800-mile trip to Waterbury, Connecticut to meet my mother and four younger siblings.

Now the unanswered questions could be asked.

But, do we really want to know the answers?

I'm sick to my stomach, and we have to stop at just about every gas station we come to.

"It's nerves," my husband says.

What will my mother look like? She's 62 years old and the only picture I have of her is on her wedding day to my dad one day before her 21st birthday.

So many times I have tried to remember her face from when we were last together. Surely when she said goodbye and tore my little baby arms from around her neck, I had burned her face into my memory. If I could just concentrate long enough to search all the old rooms of my mind, somewhere back in time there was a little room where I had placed her picture.

Fleeting pictures were always the same.

Bars across a doorway.

A baby sleeping on a mattress on the floor.

The mattress is beside a big brown desk.

A lady dressed in white sits at the desk and she is looking at me.

She has a very angry look on her face.

The bars are the rails of my crib.

I'm standing in my baby bed looking through the bars.

I am screaming for my baby sister who is on that mattress by the desk.

Grandma's stories have added to the misty memories. She said I was left alone with Sandra for long periods of time when neither of our parents could take care of us before we were put into the orphanage. I was three years old. Sandra was 18 months.

The slide show in my mind snaps me putting baby Sandra in a closet so no one would find her and take her away from me.

I'm opening a refrigerator door and taking out milk for a baby bottle. I spill it on the floor.

Baby Sandra continues crying as she hungrily sucks on the nipple.

I wrap a little blanket around her and say, "Don't cry, baby sissy."

I pull a chair to a window and look out onto a busy street.

People are everywhere but there's no one I know.

The wooden floor is bare. No toys.

Nothing for me to eat.

Baby Sissy is heavy but I try to pick her up.

The front of my shirt is all wet.

Next, I'm standing in line with other kids my age waiting for a shot.

I am glad baby sissy doesn't have to get a shot.

But nowhere in the dark recesses of my mind is that picture of our mother.

So now I'm just over 40 years old and it's only a matter of minutes until we meet our mother after all these years.

Sandra and Allison are traveling behind us. We all pull into the last filling station where we are to meet our brother Rick.

Rick has helped smooth the way for the sudden invasion of mom's past. He made it clear that our presence would create no problems because mom had told everyone about us over the years, and she had especially missed us at holiday times.

Mom has lived in the Naugatuck area all these years! She is well known in town for her involvement in community events and the Eagles' Club. She has worked at a local restaurant called "Robinson's" for many years. She isn't married but has a boyfriend named Paul. She is a grandmother. Her four grown kids were born and raised here.

Will we hug or shake hands with Rick? Does he look like either of us?

Oh, I feel like I'm going to be sick again.

A man drives up beside our car. He greets us and we fall out of the car.

Rick slowly steps out and gives us a somewhat reserved but warm embrace. Sandy snaps a picture of me greeting Rick for my scrapbook. The entourage follows Rick to his house.

At Rick's home, we meet his two sons, John and Jeff and his friendly smiling wife, Fran. They greet us and try to make us comfortable. I'm anxious to see a picture of our mother but I'm afraid to look at it. Sandra unabashedly asks if Rick has a beer and everyone has one but Bill and me. We sip a soda.

Rick says we won't see mom until later in the evening when she gets home from a trip. We try to make small talk as he shows us around the simple but well kept home and we take a walk outside. The weather is beautiful and as the evening closes in, I find it a bit chilly, so Rick loans me a jacket. The trees are starting to turn colors and I try to relax as I breathe in the autumn air. Fran has planted a small garden and the lawn is neatly mowed.

Trying to take in all I can, I notice that someone has a hobby of fixing up old cars. Rick says that would be Jeff, his oldest. John is into computer games as evidenced by the only computer in the house located next to John's bed and games scattered all around.

Family pictures in the living room leave clues about Fran's parents and baby pictures of the kids. I don't see a picture that looks like it might be our mom. Fran shows us a birthday cake she has decorated for a little girl's birthday. She enjoys doing this on the side. Rick talks about his work for the state and shows us his championship awards from playing darts.

Finally, we pile into several cars and drive only a few blocks down the street to where mom lives in a small apartment located over a pizza store. We climb the steps at the back of the building and suddenly the door opens and there stands the mystery woman who has been at the epicenter of my mind for most of my life!

"Come in," she says gently and gives us each a hug while tears run freely down our faces.

At our mother's small but cozy apartment, 22 family members gathered to celebrate the birth of a family! Cameras flash and the sound of cans snapping open fill the air. Someone brings in pizza and the place is buzzing with excited chatter and laughter.

Mom has photo albums and lots of pictures hanging everywhere. She has a few little plants in every window and the kitchen is stocked well with food. I notice her favorite perfume must be Charlie because there are several bottles in the bathroom. Perhaps the kids like to get her that for her birthday and Christmas.

We gather around the little kitchen table to show mom the letter she had sent the orphanage. She is surprised but remembers the handwritten note. Nodding her head up and down, she gets choked up trying to say that she did come back for us and we were gone.

But the night was for partying and picture taking. Our brother Billy complained that he was always the oldest until we came along and now he was someplace in the middle. The girls discussed kids, jobs and other relatives not present. We all missed the only sibling absent. Mom's firstborn, Thomas (TJ) had just joined the reserves and couldn't make the reunion.

We shared pictures and phone numbers. Little kids chased each other around the two small rooms and the guys told funny jokes and tried to catch the baseball game on TV as the Giants beat the Detroit Lions 20/0.

Every few minutes someone is making a toast to something.

We discover that Billy loves motorcycles and Rick is the best dart player in the county. Tommy is a professional roofer who scales the tall church steeples in town. Cyndi enjoys singing with mom and they have always done things together. No one had a clue that I was searching for mom or that we would ever be united.

Sandra was as proud as a Peacock to finally claim the brothers she had always wanted. Each of us found our comfort level and relaxed into the realization that we would never have to be apart again.

Our mother watched the activity of all her children and didn't say much. I noticed that she didn't drink beer but she seemed to be enjoying the activities. I wondered if she would have to clean up all this mess after we left.

Cyndi showed us her tattoos while Billy and Sandy made a bet as to who could drink the most beers. Many hours later, the fun lovers took the party to a small bar across the street and the party poopers left for a few hours of sleep. Mom's cat dashed out the front door as happy voices trailed out into the night.

The next day we visited mom's church in town and ate breakfast at Robinsons while many town folks came in to meet mom's new children. Everyone had a story to tell about our mom. She sang the National Anthem for the July 4 festivities and had been a long time participant in the annual College Capers musical program.

Too soon it was time for us to return to our respective states. Sandra would fly back to Florida. Allison would drive back to Staten Island. Bill and I would make the long trip back to Michigan. Mom promised to have a family reunion every year.

Looking back as we pulled away, I saw mom's face and her smile. I would not have to search for her any more. I could close the doors behind me and open new ones to the future of my new family.

# Chapter 45

## *We're a Family Now*

The long search for my family is finally done. Family photographs remind me that we have a link, but its strength is up to us! I wonder how many of the nine of us siblings remember all the birthdays? The purpose of this book is to help us remember. In sharing, perhaps we will become stronger.

### Thomas John
### Born June 27, 1945

Her pregnancy with Thomas was a shock to our 14-year old mother. They say Thomas was born very sick and given last rites. Lied to about his birth and raised in a school for children in New York City, one would not expect that Thomas would become one of New York City's finest - a police officer!

This writer knows little about Thomas John. We were separated when he was almost nine years old and I was three. Those childhood memories were lost in time for both of us until one day he was told that his sister, Linda, was looking for him. We celebrated a brief but joyous reunion when he was 45 years old. But he couldn't erase the painful memories, the fleeting faces in his dreams, the untold truth that had dodged him since his birth. He hasn't stayed in contact like he promised me. I don't know where he is now. I hope that time eases the pain.

Does he know that he was the one I looked for my whole life because I knew his name would not have changed? While our reunion was serendipity for me, it was a jolt into the past for him. I didn't know the pain that my efforts would cause.

I had often worried that our mother might reject us, or not want her current family to know of her past, but I hadn't given that consideration to my brother. For that, I will be forever sorry. Will I have a second chance? It's up to Thomas.

### Allison June
### Born December 7, 1945

Allison was our mother's second baby and a challenge for her family to accept. But mom didn't give up, and the family finally allowed Allison to be brought home from the hospital when she was three months old. Allison and Thomas enjoyed a sibling camaraderie while growing up. Allison became a Registered Nurse (RN) and worked on Staten Island for many years. Allison enjoys reunions with her sisters. I look forward to her rare but long telephone conversations!

### Linda Jean
### Born September 6, 1950
### Or, September 3 or 9

Serious since birth, it seems. I have always taken care of others. I'm a leader and a confident person, but I can be naïve and slow to catch on to a joke. I'm the timekeeper, the bookkeeper and the notetaker. I am the catalyst that created this civilization we call "Mom's Kids."

### Sandra Lee
### Born June 15, 1952

Sandra became my prodigy when we left the orphanage to be adopted and raised by our grandparents. Sandy could write a book on, "How To Say It" because she is the most outspoken, good times person we know. We are waiting for the family reunion when it's held at Sandy's house! She has a pool table in the living room and a spa in her back yard.

### Billy Bowden
### Born June 28, 1955

Billy always thought he was the oldest in the family until our first family reunion when there were eight of us and he

bewailed, "Now I'm somewhere in the middle!" Ha'
loyal, Billy continues to be a great part of our fam..,
love Harley Motorcycles and beer. Now it's Harleys, Fra..
grandchildren!

### Richard Bowden
### Born March 5, 1957

The scholar and family man. ~~Rick is probably~~ the most
professional~~ly educated of the family~~ and is committed to his family.
He's respected in his ~~town and works~~ hard 9-5. He enjoys sports and
hangs out with Billy a lot. Several family reunions have been held
at his home. He and I clicked immediately. You can count on us to
clean up the kitchen after each family reunion.

### Cyndi Bowden
### Born June 10, 1960

Cyndi is the only one of us five girls to have grown up knowing
our mom. Cyndi can dance like an angel and has a beautiful voice –
like our mom. She enjoys club activities with mom and appreciates
having mom close by to watch her girls grow up into beautiful young
ladies.

### Thomas Edward Harrison
### July 4, 1964

Thought he was the youngest until Pam showed up after our
first family reunion. Funny when he wants to be. Hardworking
when he chooses to be. The song, "Green, Green Grass of Home"
keeps haunting him.

### Pam
### Born 1966. Given up for adoption

The surprise to all of us. She showed up a couple months
after we found our mom. The adoption agency opened the records
so she could find her birth mother. After the first reunion, we lost
much contact with her. Hopefully, Pam is happier because she finally
found her birth mom too.

*Our Family Reunion*
*(Front, left) Sandra, Mom and Cyndi*
*(Back, left) Rick, Allison, Billy, Linda and Tommy*
*Missing are mom's oldest son, Thomas and youngest daughter, Pamela.*

# Chapter 46

## End-Of-The-Line for the "Cash Express"

**December 1, 1992**
**Dear Diary…**

"*Bill is starting to move out today. After 21 years of marriage, we have decided to separate and divorce. I'm sure the hows and whys will change over the years – in fact that is already beginning to happen. ~~For now, Bill is giddy, and I am wishing he~~ were already gone.*"

Thanksgiving this year seemed as usual to everyone but Bill and me. I knew we weren't sharing very much. He wasn't following me to bed and we weren't touching in the night. When he moved close to snuggle against my back, I remained still and quiet.

Saturday morning he got up complaining of a headache, an indication that he wouldn't be going to church. I got up and sat on the couch. He came in and sat in his usual chair. I felt a terror inside me I'd never felt before. I knew something could break the silence, or the moment could pass forever, and we would remain in our silent awful hells.

The silence broke.

"Do you have a problem?" he simply asked.

"Yes" I mumbled.

"Is it our marriage?"

"I'm so unhappy. I don't want to live like this," I answered as unchecked tears rolled down my face.

Quietly we discussed the details of a divorce as if we were discussing a long planned vacation.

My throat was so tight I could hardly speak.

I couldn't stop the constant flow of tears.

Every joint in my body was screaming with pain.

My stomach felt like someone had stuck a hot knife all the way through to my back again.

My eyes were almost swollen shut from crying and I felt so incredibly tired that I didn't know if I would still be breathing when this conversation was over.

It was the first day of the rest of my life.

## December 2 – The Second Day
## Dear Diary,

"*Bill presents me with a document that covers everything from toothbrushes to the house and cars. Questions and comments like,* 'Can I have all three TVs?'

'*My mom paid for the piano so I'll be taking it with me.*'

'*I'll take all the wedding pictures that have my family in them.*'

'~~I'd like to know if I'm leaving this relationship dirty~~ or ~~clean?~~'

*He works tirelessly at the document until the computer starts smoking and stops running. ~~It seems he's like a child in a candy~~ store ~~as he sorts and packs throughout the house.~~*

*That night he sleeps on the couch for the first time in our married life, and I take the first sleeping pill of my life.*

*Philip and Billy watch quietly from the sidelines. Phil alternating angry at me and then at his father. Billy, not giving away any emotions.*

'*Just so you're both happy,*' *he comments dryly.*"

## December 3, The Third Day
## Dear Diary,

"*I took off my ring when I went into the bank today. Bill has asked me to get a bank account without his name on it. They say I had to open a new account. I am told that I can't just take his name off.*

*I can't get the ring off either. After a minor*
*– and I feel completely naked standing there in fi*
*known for 20 years.*

*When is the right time to remove your w*.
*depends on why you put it on in the first place. I decided th*.
*(purchased myself), symbolized my struggle to make this marri*.
*work. Bill had refused to buy me a wedding band because the church*
*frowned on wearing them. Well, that fight is over.*

*All these years we have felt constrained by finances. Vacations*
*were not taken. Special items not purchased. Christmas cut back.*
*My education postponed. Funerals not attended. Major repairs not*
*done. Bills not paid on time. Oil not changed on the car. Carpets not*
*cleaned. Nursing shoes worn to a frazzle. Haircuts delayed and choice*
*foods avoided. Suddenly, with one word, it seems, we can afford for*
*Bill to get an apartment in South Bend, and he is able to free himself*
*of all these obligations that have hung around our necks like a noose*
*all these years. I'm confused."*

*Each of us working hard in the daily*
*Struggle to keep up & stay together*

### December 4, The Fourth Day

Freedom has many meanings. I wake this morning and
think of what I will be free to do that didn't seem so free before. I
make a list and write in my diary.

### Dear Diary,

*"Suddenly I can think about what is real inside of me. I can do*
*all these things and not fear criticism or rebuke.*

*To play my flute*
*To sing while I do dishes*
*To laugh out loud*
*To dream of freedom*
*To cherish my body*
*To cry at a sad song*
*To protect my soul*
*To dance in the street*
*To walk without fear*
*To sleep in peace*
*To wake with joy."*

The ring-mark is still on my finger. I try to rub it away. I
still feel exposed, but I feel so much peace inside. Bill wants to be

*Each wisely for love + acceptance +*

late "for old times sake" and I refuse. Have I ever refused him? t's a question I'll never have to debate again!

## The Evening of the Fourth Day.
## Dear Diary...

"Bill finished moving out today. I was trying to type a term paper for Philip before his Christmas Party at 5:30 p.m. and Bill was rushing around moving out the couch and chairs, the TVs, the piano, the bed, books and bookcases, clothes, dishes, linens and household supplies. He took a load to South Bend and returned about 8 p.m. to help finish up Philip's paper.

We eat supper at Pizza Hut and he talks non-stop. He is mindless of the cold pizza on my plate. "This is a relief after 21 years of an emotional rollercoaster," he exclaims.

He glances at the waitress and says in a low voice to me, "I'm fortunate to know so many single eligible, educated women."

He compliments himself for being in such good shape and boasts, 'Women will be falling all over me.' He knocks on the table as he talks of how we, 'have done this and still remained friends.' He thanks me for being so, 'unselfish with everything' and for helping make the transfer, 'smooth.'

I listen and, as usual, he fails to notice that I haven't said a word.

Bill's brother called tonight. It was interesting to hear Bill explain, 'Why Linda did this'. Mostly, he said it was because of my financial independence. 'She makes more than I do and that was the final straw,' he told his brother.

When he was packing up the last bag to leave at 11 p.m. and I was wondering how awkward his final good-by would be, the phone rang! It was Kephart Cottage with a patient who was running a very high blood pressure and showing signs of a stroke.

I waved Bill out the door and toward his car. He pulled away with his usual good-by honk on the horn, and I was suddenly alone in an almost empty house."

I sit down on the only chair in the empty living room surrounded by deafening silence. The couch smells musty, but it's the dogs' favorite chair so Bill has left it for them.

Now it's time to find the person inside of
will let someone else take control of my life be'
to find out who I am.  Less than a week ago I ha.
another chance.  Now I'm afraid to move from this ı.
couch for fear I will lose what I have.   I can't bring mysei.
bed. I'm free, but I'm truly alone, as I know I will be for many ı.
times in the months to come.  I sneeze and it echoes through the
house.

## December 5, The Fifth Day

I wake.  The first drug-free awakening since we agreed to get
a divorce.  I take a moment to give my life a word.  I decide the word
is, "joy."  That's not the same as "happy."  Joy is the inner glow of
happiness about to burst into flame.

***Dear Diary...***

*"Today I will tear through all my dresser drawers, the closets,
the storage in the basement and the boys' room.  I will toss out anything
that has an unhappy memory attached to it.  I must decide how to go
about the business of this divorce – but at least I can spell the word
now! Tomorrow is trash day!"*

# Chapter 47

## Who Was Linda Cash?

My boys must be thinking, "What's mom going to write about dad?"

After all, Bill Cash and I were married for over 21 years. We married when I was 20-years old and a few days past graduating from school as a Licensed Practical Nurse. We divorced when I was 42-years old. He had his PhD and I was still a hard working LPN.

Bill was a senior at Southern College, Collegedale, TN back in 1969 when we met at my first alumni homecoming at Laurelbrook School. After a long alumni-hosted afternoon walk, he asked me to be his steady girl, and we said an emotional good-by at the airport as I left to return to LPN school in Dayton, Ohio.

We planned the wedding while I was away at school. We got married upon my return during his spring break on March 9, 1971 in Graysville, Tennessee not far from Laurelbrook School.

Grandpa Mascunana was so proud to walk me down the aisle. He was, after all, my legal father. Everyone was a happy family on that day.

We lived in ten different houses and four states, during our many years together. Bill narrowly missed being drafted for the Vietnam War by one number, and continued to complete his advanced education during most of those 21 years.

Two sons blessed our home within the first five years. Both pregnancies caused me to be incredibly sick with nausea and I was hospitalized several times, but I always bounced back quickly after holding my babies in my arms.

In the end, Bill told me I was still the loving sweet person he had married but we had grown apart in too many ways. Whatever we saw in each other on that alumni reunion day wasn't enough to keep us whole for all those years.

As usual in a split of parents, and to the regret of both Bill and me, our boys got hurt the most by our divorce. They are good sons who didn't choose sides and continue to love each us very much.

A few days ago I was chatting long distance to Neil Hunt. He has been a mutual friend since we were at Laurelbrook. Neil commented that the hardest part about the divorce was not seeing Bill and me together. It seemed that we had always been together! We had created a family civilization, and I'm sure our family and friends were just as perplexed as to why we split up and how to react as our boys were.

Philip recently reminded me that both of us (his parents) have changed over the years, having learned lessons from the past. My wise son said when a relationship is in trouble, "both feel the hurt of it."

Having said that, we did have lots of good times and carried on a fairly normal existence as a family. I think what held us together the most was our affiliation with the Seventh-day Adventist church. We were both leaders and contributed in many ways especially to the Eau Claire SDA Church and School in Eau Claire, Michigan.

As the boys got older, I followed them through each little Sabbath School department leading out in the Kindergarten, Junior and other classes. I often played the piano or told stories from the Bible or provided activities. And, I always enjoyed being with my boys!

I still recall fondly the times Bill and I provided special music at church services with him at the piano and me playing the flute. We played, "The Holy City" to hushed audiences and it still chills me to remember how well we did that together! It is such a majestic song!

But, deep down I didn't feel comfortable with Bill and perhaps he didn't with me.

We never took the time to really know the true person inside each other and ourselves. My low self-esteem and his "know-all" attitude didn't help. I felt that it was impossible for me to make him happy no matter how hard I tried to please him.

My cooking wasn't good enough. I didn't control spending the way I should. I didn't keep up with him socially and I couldn't say no when others asked for my help.

Eventually Grandma Mascunana needed medical care that I could give. I was the only family member who couldn't say, "no" and who didn't distance themselves from her. All of her four birth children kept their distance and took no responsibility for her care.

Eventually, she moved to a nearby retirement home and demanded constant medical care due to diabetes and obesity. Her constant needs took much of the very limited time that I had with my family. I was working 16-18 hours a day as a nurse and even then we couldn't pay all the bills. Grandma also continued to be ungrateful and inconsiderate of my feelings.

As we discussed our divorce proceedings, Bill asked me to admit fault and file for divorce so his reputation would remain good in the church – assuming that I didn't intend to continue as a member of the SDA church - and also assuming I wouldn't mind being singled out as a wrongdoer.

Because I was feeling the frustration that had surfaced so many times with grandma, I could see a way out and was finally able to walk away. He wasn't a bad man, just someone I couldn't live with and continue breathing! The final good-by was benevolent and complete.

We decided to divorce a few weeks after I won the election for township clerk. I think he was shocked that I had won! His comment was that having won the election, I would be able to take care of myself and perhaps wouldn't feel abandoned if we divorced. He knew my biggest fear in life was that I'd be left all alone again.

I was afraid that we would get divorced but he would still continue to control me, so I wanted a clean break. I was also concerned that he would consider me "clingy" as he had referred to me that way at times.

Obviously, I wanted to live my life my way.

Bill didn't want me to continue a close relationship with his mother who always said I was like a daughter she never had. His mother and I respected Bill's wishes for several years, but we still send birthday and Christmas cards. She will always get a call from me on Mother's Day.

I was careful to disassociate myself from his dad who had always been very kind to me. I'm glad today we keep in contact and visit when we are in the area.

In the end, I did have an empty nest, but I discovered that I was stronger than I thought!

Today, many years after our divorce, Bill is probably as happy as he will ever be and I am happier than I have ever been.

Sometimes I wonder what would have happened to me if I hadn't married so soon after getting my LPN course and finally being free of grandma's constant control. Back then I was still very naive and insecure. I may still have some of those traits, but hopefully in a more mature way.

One must always look forward and use past experiences to learn and grow.

*This book is a reflection of my life's path, to leave a legacy for those who knew and loved me.*

# Chapter 48

## If I Can't Do Great Things...

I encourage everyone to think about *what and who* creates within you feelings of cheer and satisfaction. It occurs to me that I am the best person in the world to appreciate my past accomplishments, reflect on my brightest joys and plan my future goals. So, let's get started!

Becoming a Registered Nurse has always been an off and on goal. Even after being an LPN for 35 years, I still sign up at the local college for RN classes! On the other hand, I'm such a good LPN that I wonder if could be a better RN. Just to walk across a platform in a graduation gown would be something I know I'd feel very good about.

My really happiest moments are when I'm going to school, having to read books and take tests to challenge myself! I regret that my education has always taken a back seat, because choosing what I want has always been difficult for me. I'm usually helping others; cheering them on to what's next! I should have gotten more education because it's such a "high" for me and I would have made such good use of it. Maybe it will still happen. If I were rich, I'd spend more time in school!

While we lived in Michigan and the boys were small, I was a correspondent for The Herald-Palladium in St. Joseph, Michigan. I learned how it feels to be filled with ambition, confidence and purpose. Those eight years were crazy because I ran after every fire, accident and unusual event in our town 24/7 except when I was working as a nurse in another town. I covered town meetings and school board meetings as a reporter and could quote every word. I enjoyed writing about people and telling their stories.

I couldn't have been such a successful correspondent without my longsuffering, chain-smoking editor, Tom Brundrett. He taught me everything about journalism and computers at the time. We spent so much time together that our spouses were jealous but they needn't have worried. I was known as a fair and honest reporter and was always respected by the officials in our town.

Teaching CPR for the American Red Cross and volunteering at special events in our county was exciting for me. I also worked closely with the firemen and policemen keeping them all updated in CPR. I don't think my teenage Billy appreciated my close association with the local police at the time, but he knew I looked forward to teaching those classes.

Photography developed from a sense of wanting to start my own business and make money at it. My diary reflects how scared I was to take that step to order the studio equipment. I remember the day it arrived, I cried because I thought I'd never be able to understand the f-stops and shadows and light placements. But, I became one of the best wedding photographers in the county, and shared that business with Billy and Philip. They often helped me with setting up the studio and accompanied me on weddings. I still shoot weddings but have left the studio work behind for a while.

Friends pushed me into studying for the ham radio license. I was sure I'd never pass something like that but wanted to enter into the world of electronics and amateur radio. Today I'm proud of that license and plan to join a radio club in Columbus, Ohio.

It can be a rather expensive hobby and I don't have much equipment but it's a fun experience I look forward to. I'm looking for a service oriented radio club.

Winning an elected position on our township and becoming the township clerk probably was the catalyst for my divorce from Bill Cash but something I treasure very much!

About then I also took the emergency medical technician course (EMT) so I could volunteer for the local ambulance service. I considered becoming a paramedic but discovered that my body mechanics were not good enough to protect my back while lifting heavy people and big stretchers. Working as an EMT was short-lived, but I look back at that experience with satisfaction and pride.

My work with handicapped children at the county school for MRDD was very gratifying. I loved every child and knew each of the 250 little ones by name and history. They taught me about being positive no matter what the handicap, enjoying life no matter what the challenge, and the pure pleasure of little accomplishments!

There's a small picture on the wall by my bathroom light switch that says,

**"If I can't do great things, I will do small things in a great way."**

With only a few months of formal music lessons, I can enjoy playing the piano, the organ, the flute and the accordion. My poetry has been published and my photos have won awards. I have traded on e-bay and learned how to post on the World-Wide Web. With little education, I've been a successful entrepreneur and business owner.

It is *beyond imagination* what I would be doing today if I had 18-20 years of education like I helped provide for Bill and my boys. Certainly I would not be working in a nursing home passing medications with no input into making things better.

*My nursing dream is to* be part of a creative team helping to make whatever I'm doing far better than it was when I got there.

Photography still holds a special place in my heart. Someday I will once again bring smiles to life and create magic in my "Magic Moments" studio!

Proof of what can happen if I'm given the opportunity to shine is my history with Teresa's Country Homes in Berrien Springs. Because Teresa is a very smart and talented businesswoman, the 40-bed homes prospered and she was able to move to sunny Florida and leave the day-to-day management of the homes to me. I worked closely with her administrative assistant, Marian Mendel, to keep the homes above census and citation-free for several years. I really loved the employees, some of whom will read this story. Marian is a jewel of a woman. I appreciate the trust Teresa had in me and will never forget what I learned about being a good leader.

Most of all, I want to keep looking for ways to improve and grow in spirit and to keep looking for those golden nuggets life hides in the most unexpected places!

Past mistakes still haunt me. Sometimes I have nightmares that I have comm. the unpardonable sin by writing this BK. at the x, I thought it was important to tell it like I saw it, but, as some have said, "It's in the eyes of the beholder."

# Chapter 49

### *Nostrils flaring...*

On the sixth day after Bill moved out, I came home from the township hall at noon to take out the trash. Reluctant for the neighbors to see how much I was tossing out, my plan was to get it out to the curb while most were at work.

In the midst of my hurried trips with boxes of discards from Bill and remnants of a civilization that would never live in that house again, I paused as a car drove slowly by. He looked like someone I knew. Why it was....Doc Stowe!

During the stress of the past few months I had returned for chiropractic care and had confided that things were more stressful than usual. He assumed that the effects of the campaign had taken their toll, and congratulated me on winning a hard fought election.

Not only was I working as administrator of Teresa's Country Homes with the challenges of 42 senior residents, but also I was learning the ropes of running a township as a member of the board and manager of the election process. Now in the middle of a divorce, I seemed to be in overload!

Added to the mushrooming legal battles, Bill had put the numbers together and filed for me to pay him child support for Philip who was 16 years old. It seems that even with his PhD, I was making more money than he was, and he couldn't resist taking advantage of that legal loophole.

But on that cloudy afternoon, Doc Stowe said he just wanted to check on how I was doing, and he invited me to eat a home cooked meal at his farm. He said he was sure that I could use a break.

Soon his "checking up" became more frequent. The trips to the farm after a long day at both jobs was refreshing and the quiet evenings at his place replaced the bustling, almost frantic schedule I'd been accustomed to – now all gone – at my house.

I still hadn't learned that women who are not sure of their inner self are surrounded with an invisible aura that is recognizable by those men who can sense the perfume of insecurity, the whiff of despair and the whisper of indecision.

Nostrils flaring, they react to the unspoken body language, ambience, mannerisms and demeanor of one who is not strong and in control.

I reacted. He responded. It took several months for me to realize that something was not completely right.

One morning I woke up at his place to find tire tracks in the snow right up to the bedroom window. Someone wasn't happy, and I knew it wasn't a stranger in the night who had pulled up to try and spy on us – or send him a message!

Bill wasn't pleased about the relationship and asked Philip to move to South Bend with him even though it meant the 30-mile drive back and forth to school and separation from all his friends.

It took a little longer for me to realize that Doc Stowe didn't want our relationship public knowledge. He didn't want to be seen with me in town and didn't talk about our friendship in the office. When we went out to eat, he drove to another town. He always wanted me to visit at his place. I was confused but emotionally restrained by a man with grips of steel and a heart encased in stone.

Eventually I discovered that he was still in a relationship with a woman he was seeing when he first drove by my house! When I asked questions, he put me off. When I found out about the woman, he denied it.

I was devoted to a man who couldn't make a commitment, wouldn't promise me a future and choked on the most precious words a woman wants to hear.

The years of emotional distress and lack of tender affection had created an indigence that silenced the inner voice of reason and truth!

I continued existing in an emotional limbo, a fool's paradise, convincing my sons, family and friends that I was happy. I went to work every day with a smile and cheerfulness while hiding a pain so great it cannot be put into words that others would believe.

Some find it incomprehensible that I took out a $25,000 second mortgage on my house to pay off his back taxes and a $10,000 debt owned to his daughter.

My life with Stowe was a three-year ordeal that is recorded to the smallest details in my ever-faithful diary.

I played the greatest act on earth – and few noticed how perfectly it was performed!

# Chapter 50

## *Rebound Cheater*

He was going hunting again. Pulling on the triple layered jumpsuit I had painstakingly made the previous spring and tugging at his new hunting boots, his eyes didn't have that usual bright shine of enthusiasm that precedes deer season. Picking up the thermos of strong hot coffee and stuffing a few sandwiches into a brown bag he would leave in the truck so the scent wouldn't scare off the big white buck he was looking for, he paused.

The pickup was loaded. He had packed the beautiful deer quilted blanket I had sewed together that summer in anticipation of the winter hunts. His favorite bottle of female deer scent was ready.

The old treestand had been dragged out and placed high in a favorite tree close to the edge of a meadow he had been watching all summer. We had walked the woods together for months following deer tracks, searching for evidence of the big bucks that roamed the Michigan woods.

Suddenly, he pulled out a chair from the kitchen table and sat down with a deep sigh.

"It's not working," he said. "I know something must be wrong with me, but I'm not able to make a commitment. I don't know why. I won't be back after this hunt."

With a heavy heart, I slowly eased into a chair across from him. Why did I know this was coming? I had refused to believe he couldn't return the feelings I had for him and that he wasn't loyal to the unspoken commitment we had shared for the last few years.

Yes, immediately after the divorce, I had jumped into this relationship with Doc Stowe. His wife had recently passed away and each of us should have taken time to heal, but both of us were lonely and vulnerable.

Likewise, we were also respected professionals in our town and we should have known better. He was the local chiropractor and I was the township clerk – having recently won that elected position. I was also working at Teresa's Country Homes during that time.

But sometimes sadness makes one defenseless.

Kindness feels strong and secure to a broken heart.

He had given me a gentleness I had never experienced. He seemed to read my mind when I felt afraid. He took time to be with me like no one else had ever done. We let the wind blow in our face on long motorcycle rides, camping trips alone and long, quiet walks together.

But, he could never say the words, "I love you."

Now, I knew the truth was looming in my face although I had struggled with the suspicion for some time. I had avoided surprising him at his office because I felt that something was hiding there he didn't want me to know.

Sometimes he got late night calls and had to leave to "adjust a sick patient" even though I knew that chiropractic adjustments are not instant health.

He often spent many hours "in the woods" when I knew his truck was not parked near his hunting grounds. He brought me too many gifts.

I had often prayed that he would be able to say those magic words I needed to hear. It was difficult to tell him how much I wanted him, when doing so sounded like I was begging.

I silently pleaded for his mind to open up and let me get closer to his heart.

Many times he needed space alone and I respected that although I wondered if I was the fool and how long I would be able to fruitlessly tap on the glass wall that surrounded him and his heart.

Looking at the sadness in his face and feeling the pain in mine, I had to ask, "Is there someone else?"

He nodded and answered, "Yes, I've been seeing someone, but not anyone you know."

My intuition had been right. It has always been strength within me and I should have listened long before now.

He got up and walked out the door. As he turned and looked back at me the last time his voice broke as he simply said, "I love you."

I stood. Totally confused. Usually strong and confident and slow to anger, I felt stunned and sickened to my stomach. I knew his words didn't match his actions. I thought of all the hours I had spent sewing for his upcoming hunting season.

I wanted to run and grab my beautiful quilt from the truck. I didn't want his two-timing hands touching it.

By the way, the new truck he was driving was in my name! Had he considered that?

With a deep feeling of dread, I wondered if Stowe would recognize the huge debt he owed me. He had refused to sign any legal documentation for the $25,000 loan saying I should trust him to be good for it.

He knew I had kept fastidious documentation on what he had paid back so far, but I wondered if that would be any good now.

But there was a part of me that felt crushed and hurt. As I watched the taillights turn left- away from the hunting grounds and into the arms of another woman - I rushed to the bathroom and turned on the shower to hide the sound of my screams and flood of tears.

For several days I hardly left the bathroom. I was alone in the house. I felt like my two boys were all I had left in the world. My precious, hardworking sons who were doing so well in high school and college. I didn't think I had the courage to tell them what a fool I had been.

The last three years had been a seesaw of highs and lows. Doc had never really let go of his last "girlfriend" who ran into me at the gas station with a replica of Doc's favorite leather jacket on and the twin logo of an eagle on the sleeve. She had told me that she and Doc still saw each other, "but not in this town," as if that would make it acceptable.

His relationship with his daughter and her husband who was also a chiropractor was very rocky and I was frequently caught in the middle of their disagreements or she totally ignored me altogether. They had long periods of not speaking to each other even though she was supposedly running the office.

She didn't want me around when she was with her dad. They had Christmas in his office and I was not invited even though I had spent literally hundreds of dollars on gifts for their child.

I was not immune to his infidelities and poor communication abilities, but chose to ignore any area that might "rock the boat".

I let him and his daughter have their space at my expense.

Anytime I dared suggest making a formal commitment to our relationship, I suffered *his* silence for days on end when he wouldn't talk to me and I held my disappointment and frustration inside when he would not even say that he loved me.

My hold was so tight that I nearly lost my bearings when he walked out. I had thought I could change him into an intimate partner who would be true blue to me. I thought if I was good enough and patient enough, he would change into someone I could trust with my heart.

The most difficult lesson in life is learning that you cannot change anyone. It is not fair to them or to you. Your emotional heart will die long before your physical heart stops beating!

So he walked out and I started walking all night long. I went to the St. Joseph River that ran through our town.

Following the fisherman's trails by moonlight, I beat myself without mercy for getting so involved with someone unwilling to be a true partner.

I grieved for my dashed dreams and hopes for a relationship filled with freedom and joy. I worried that I would be alone for the rest of my life – not good enough for any man. I was most disappointed in myself.

Feeling lifeless and looking pale and haggard, I struggled to be a confident nurse and elected official during the day.

It seemed like a lifetime of grief before I looked in the mirror one morning and said what my friends had been thinking. "You need to pull yourself together!" He was out enjoying his freedom and I was wasting precious time.

I had continued my childhood survival mode of taking care of others and putting myself last hoping that would be enough.

After Bill had moved out, he had moved into my house in town and sold his large farmhouse with many acres of prime woods.

I spent weeks cleaning out his large farmhouse and getting it ready for sale. I sifted through all his dead wife's belongings not knowing if I should laugh or cry.

Later, when he moved to a larger chiropractic office, I worked tirelessly to fix up the new office he purchased. I organized all his personal and patient files and got my accountant to settle up years of back taxes.

Every day I left my job at the township hall or the assisted living facility at noon to run home and fix him a warm meal. I washed and ironed his shirts and bought new clothes to match his "new style." Evenings were spent not with my friends or interests but watching TV with him.

When I got sunburned on motorcycle trips, he thought it was funny. When I limped in pain from the hurt of miles of walking in the woods tracking deer, he said I needed more adjustments. He talked vulgar in front of his friends and was ruthless with my emotions but made fun of me for protesting. To my disgust, he flirted with wildly most all the women, but threw it back in my face when I complained.

But most importantly, I had been blinded by my feelings when I should have seen things more clearly and acted smarter. I lost crucial time that should have been spent with my boys after the divorce when they were hurting too.

Now I had to get on with my life. My sons needed a strong mother who could take care of herself. I needed a helpmate and a loving partner the boys and I could all appreciate!

# Chapter 51

## Old Ghosts and Good Friends!

Two of my best friends and closest confidents were Sue at the township hall and Marian at Teresa's Country Homes. They offered unconditional support and listened to my confessions of despair and grief during my incredibly sad and painful experience when Doc left.

It was difficult to explain why I had to move on. By now there were too many "ghosts" in my house in Berrien Springs. No one knew how desperately I needed to move out of that house.

Every time I heard the dripping of the kitchen sink during the night, I was painfully reminded that I had no one to fix such a simple nuisance.

As winter neared, I worried about how I would get the snow removed from the driveway. Bill was the only one who had known how to start the "keyless" snow blower.

The air conditioner was on its last leg – so said the repairman when it went out last summer. The condensation pipe kept clogging up and water always backed up into the furnace which was a little un-nerving for me too!

The roof was starting to leak so badly that I had certain buckets set aside and marks on the floor where to put them when it rained – and a new roof had not solved the leaking problem!

My heart stopped every time I flushed the commode and it didn't go down right away. I had no idea how to stop an overflowing commode!

The sump pump in the basement for the washer had a plastic bucket over the top so the water from the shower wouldn't splash on it and burn it out as had happened once when Bobby was taking a shower. I didn't want to be near it when it chugged and slurped up the wash water.

The house had too many reminders of others who had lived there and moved on, leaving me behind.

The 20x30 framed family portrait that nobody wanted. The wedding album I couldn't bear to take apart. A box of old letters from Bill, sent while I was in nursing school. And, my long sparkling wedding dress that I had carried around for almost 25 years!

Then there were the holes in the wall of the garage where Doc target practiced from the roadway to the back yard. The back yard was littered with discarded deer targets and a weed covered flowerbed that hadn't been planted for several years.

The deer head mounted over the fireplace was now repulsive!

The back bedroom was unusable because it had been redesigned into a gunroom and bullet-making factory.

Coffee stains on the tables – and I didn't drink coffee.

Large hooks in the garage for hanging dead deer and blood marks on the garage floor that reminded me of the day Doc handed me a quivering heart to hold in my hand. He said he was proud of me for not throwing up.

I didn't even have my old furniture to feel familiar with. The piano that calmed me on quiet evenings was gone. My ham radio had been sold. It held such a strange fascination for me and gave me a sense of pride when I answered roll call on Wednesday nights for severe weather preparedness. I didn't even have a CD player anymore or a stereo to enjoy the classical and flute music I loved.

The big TV sitting on the bedroom dresser had an ugly chip in one corner of the screen. It was an awkward reminder that what had hit the screen had been directed at Doc's head during one of many fights with his wife.

The couch smelled like cigarette smoke and the carpet smelled like Muffy.

When a few of the single SDA men started stopping by or calling for one reason or another, I was sure I didn't want to stir up any more local ghosts to occupy my house!

So, much to Sue and Marian's concern, I signed up with a matching service on the computer.

Instead of walking the riverbanks at night, I now stayed up surfing for someone who would match the profile I had posted.

# Chapter 52

## 99 Percent Angel

"*Watching the geese fly south with their mates and listening to their sounds of pleasure, I ponder whether I will ever find someone to Light Up My Life. I'm a nurse, professional photographer and elected official in the town where I live near the shores of Lake Michigan. I'm ambitious, optimistic, healthy and mobile (able to relocate).*

*A few qualities that would make my life complete: Someone educated but not an educated fool. Polite, but not overly so. Doesn't mind if I can't dance and doesn't mind the silence sometimes. Tolerates cats and loves big dogs. Has the ability to turn his socks inside out. Must believe in God or Innate. Must be excited about life and happy within his heart. Doesn't require five TV sets on a Sunday afternoon. Can commit to honesty, integrity and ME! Loves to listen to an angel babble when she's happy. If I can trust you with my heart! Those few men who qualify for at least nine out of ten, please write immediately. The geese are almost ready for winter and I am not.*"

I'm sure my dusty old guardian angel had something to do with directing me to the posting Jim had placed on Match.com.

# Chapter 53

## Man of Many Seasons

"A man who has journeyed 198 seasons living west of the sunrise and east of the sunset seeks a good woman for email, pen pal, or long-term relationship.

A quiet envisionary, gentle and sensitive, emotionally strong and physically capable, man-of-many-meanings with the power, force and direction to mutually share a meaningful destiny; is looking for a good marriage-minded woman (if that's what you want) with the honorable intention of friendship, courtship and marriage (if that's what you want), family and a lifetime of fulfillment.

Educated in the universities and schooled in the ways of life. Knowledge obtained through discipline. Patience gained by understanding. Compassion achieved through personal suffering. A giver of my all and nurturer of much. Gentle by word and touch. A seeker of truth and meaning in experience and conversation.

In the meaning of your womanhood, you will be romantic and easygoing, beautiful within yourself, hold value to the fulfillment that a man can grant. Does not want to stand in his shadow but in our sunlight. Enjoyments: Dancing under the stars, reading, fireside companionship, playing in life's sandbox, flowers, music and cheesecake...Willing to travel to your backyard, sit a spell and speak of our mutual destiny.... Walks upright, no tail, lifetime guarantee on all moving parts and battery. Children from a previous relationship very acceptable. Come take my hand and let us walk..."

Jim's response was different from a few other guys I had been corresponding with. He didn't ask for a picture, nor did he seem overly interested in my measurements!

He wrote as one who would be more interested in giving my kitty a dish of warm milk than wanting to meet me at a fancy restaurant.

He wrote, *"One does not discard the emotion of hurt from any experience. But it must be placed into proper meaning and understood. It is out of any emotional hurt that we learn better to love unconditionally, give for the greater love of the other. Then we release all our 'baggage' and it sinks to the bottom of the sea as we rise above."*

*...A Meow to you Samantha*

How could I not help but encourage someone who writes:

*"I want to calm your 'afraid' feelings. I am a quiet, gentle, calm, perceiving of my environs, a caring and loving man. I am not looking to 'take from' but to give."*

I had to smile when Jim wrote me after telling his son, John about our friendship. "John had a smirk on his face when I told him of you. 'She lives where? I never know what you're saying half the time with your writing. About damn time you found yourself a good woman!'"

Every time I turned on the computer, Jim's words poured out in simple verse.

*At touch of verse*
*And if I may,*
*A cyber kiss on forehead*
*To send you on your way.*
*"Can love be locked away and kept hid?*
*Yes and it gathers dust and mildew*
*And shrivels itself in shadows*
*Unless it learns the sun can help.*
*Snow, rain, storms can help.*
*Birds in their one-room family nests*
*Shaken by winds cruel and crazy – they can all help.*
*Lock not away your love nor keep it hid..."*

# The Rose

Some say love, it is a river, that drowns the tender reed
Some say love, it is a razor, that leaves your soul to bleed
Some say love, it is a hunger, an endless aching need
I say love, it is a flower, and you, its only seed

It's the heart afraid of breaking, that never learns to dance
It's the dream afraid of waking, that never takes the chance
It's the one who won't be taken, the one who can't seem to give
And the soul afraid of dying, that never learns to live

When the night has been too long and the road has been too long
And you think that love is only for the lucky and the strong
Just remember that in the winter, far beneath the bitter snow
Lies the seed that with the sun's love in the spring, becomes the
Rose.

~Bette Midler

# Chapter 54

## *Highlander Hawk Follows*
## *Call of the Geese*

The "Highlander Hawk" married his "99 Percent Angel" in a magnificent sunrise ceremony overlooking the shores of Lake Michigan 55 days later. A few brave friends and our children assembled with us at the lakeside beachhouse in Bridgman, Michigan for the chilly early morning ceremony complete with a bagpiper, hot chocolate and wedding cake.

My marriage to this stranger from out of town was a shock to the entire town, my friends, relatives and family. Those who know me trusted me. Those who didn't, enjoyed the juicy gossip for a while.

I can assure you that my intuition and perception about Jim was accurate. He is devoted, loyal and faithful. His tender consideration of my feelings and watchfulness for my well-being continues to amaze me.

I chose to leave my town and all my friends to go and live with Jim in his city. I gave up my home, my well-known status in town and a nursing job that I loved more than any job I'd ever had. But, I have no regrets.

True to his word, he is a gentle man of many meanings. He still gives the black cat a tiny dish of warm milk every night. He loves to walk our golden retriever in the fields across the road as he carries her bottle of water and water dish on his belt. He knows how to fix a dripping faucet, change the oil in the car and how to replace a roof on a house.

When a storm approaches, Jim hurries to the porch to watch the rain. He has been caught washing dishes in the dark. He doesn't mix the whites and darks and remembers the fabric softener. My birthdays are never forgotten, and the beautiful clothes he gets for me always fit!

If he uses my car, I can expect to find it filled with gas. If I work late, he and Sheba (my dog) wait by the window for me to get home.

A kind and gentle man, Jim is also a proud Vietnam Vet. He assures me that if I ever give the nudge of approval, he will collect on the $12,522.99 personal debt still owed to me by Stowe.

We've had more life experiences in our eight years together than most have in a lifetime because we are not afraid to take chances and get out of our comfort zone!

After our marriage, we relocated to Ohio because he had the more stable state job, but I continued to commute 300 miles to Michigan for weekend weddings and township clerk responsibilities until my term expired.

Because of my extensive travel, I was doing private duty nursing during the week in Columbus for a particular nursing case, but the family was frustrated because the agency I worked for didn't always provide dependable coverage.

One day I proposed that if we started our own nursing agency, we could hire nurses to provide around the clock care and guarantee coverage because I could go in myself if needed.

So, Jim and I developed a nursing agency called Angelwings Health Care Services. The agency was something we both contributed to, and it kept us very busy for almost a year until the family no longer needed our services. At that point, we decided that life is too short to be so incredibly busy 24/7.

It is proof that with my entrepreneur spirit and Jim's business expertise, we are a good team and can work hand in hand together.

Later, we successfully operated a large children's photography business while in the process of purchasing the studio. We held on to it long enough for me to discover how much I love being a professional photographer and how natural I am at taking photographs.

Regrettably, after a few months, the owners backed out of the deal and closed down the business. The experience was a golden

moment in time that also proved to be a confidence b...
I'm glad we were not afraid to take the chance to do ...
love.

Our biggest and most challenging decision was for Jim to quit his state job and for us to relocate to Florida in 2002, where it was our plan to settle down near Sandra and her husband in Tampa. While some may say we made a mistake, we don't agree.

Sandra and Craig have spent a lifetime establishing a nice home and good jobs, but we just couldn't find our niche. The weather was hotter than I remembered. The houses weren't up to my standards for what we could pay. Nursing jobs were more competitive. Jim couldn't get back in with a state job as he had been led to believe.

Our dogs were always hot and the hurricanes seemed to take a special interest in our back yard! Jim missed his Ohio Valley and Sandra encouraged me to do whatever would be happiest for me. So we bit the bullet and came back home where the leaves turn colors in the fall and snow covers the fields in the winter.

Arriving to a new 2-bedroom apartment on a cold blustery winter day, we were grateful for Jim's son John, and his strong back to help unload the 24-foot U-Haul truck. He had taken a bus to Tampa, helped packed the truck and then drove 2,000 miles to Ohio and with superhuman effort, unloaded most everything for us.

We arrived in Columbus a few days before Christmas without a penny in our pocket. No Christmas tree. Very little food, and no gifts to share! But, we had each other and a strong faith that something good would happen soon.

John was happy to have us back in Ohio so he could introduce his wife, Denise, and our first grandchild to us for the first time! Baby Victoria was a surprise to everyone when she was born unexpectedly at home on News Year's Eve of 2003. No one knew that Denise was pregnant!

Denise was excited to meet her new mother-in-law (me!) and to discover that I love her as my own. Her life is a special story waiting to be written also! I hope Denise will always remember that I love her 100 percent!

On Christmas Eve, I sewed a wolf quilt for Jim and he bought me a pair of gloves and some warm socks. After the New Year, ne started putting his resume everywhere he could, and I started working two nursing jobs to help get us on our feet again.

We carried a heavy load of worry and fear but tried to encourage each other that things would get better soon.

As this book goes to press, over a year later, Jim is still putting in applications, getting job interviews for jobs that don't get filled due to budget cuts, and working with a headhunter who isn't giving us our money's worth! But we persevere and don't look back or give up! We still have each other and our strong love to get us through.

Jim often reminds me that I have an angel on my shoulder who continues to watch over me, and he sometimes asks my angel to watch over him too.

Jim encourages me to do anything that makes me happy – and honestly means it! I am finally able to pull out all the old diaries and write my book without fear of critical assessments on every word!

I am not encumbered with depression and grief. Oh yes, there are challenges to confront and day-to-day problems to solve, but my heart is at peace knowing I have a mate whom I can trust with my heart and with my dreams!

I know that I am loved unconditionally and forever. It is with pride and pleasure that Jim tells me he loves me every day of my life.

My children cherish and love me and would be at my side in a moment if I called. Sandra is a happily married woman and only a phone call away!

The mystery of our mother has been solved and we keep in touch.

My husband today thinks I am more of an angel than I really am. He brings me purpose and vision.

We look forward to the next 55 years with confidence, optimism and contentment.

# Chapter 55

## Celestial Numbers and Golden Nuggets

Jim has always dreamed numbers and they have had a special meaning in his lifetime. A few weeks before we met on the Internet, Jim had fallen asleep while waiting for the evening news. Suddenly, he woke up with a start like someone had touched his shoulder. The clock read, 11:55. He had missed the news, so he got ready and went to bed. Later, he woke up again with the feeling of a touch on his shoulder. It was 12:55. Then again, with the awareness of urgency, he woke up and looked at the clock. All night long he awoke at 1:55, 2:55, 3:55 and 5:55. After that, he got up and lit a white candle thinking that might help to make this stop, but the next few days he was flooded with the number 55 in his accounting work and everyplace he turned. He was frustrated and mystified.

Several nights later, he was wakened several times with the same urgent feeling. As he sometimes does when numbers seem meaningful, he wrote the times down not having a clue what they might mean. 1:07, 2:19, 3:20 and 5:04.

On our honeymoon, Jim let out a gasp of surprise when I happened to mention that we had gotten married 55 days after we first started writing. The number had not come up before our wedding, and Jim had not realized the significance until I made the comment!

With that in mind, Jim pulled out a piece of paper from his billfold. Listed were the numbers he had written during the nights when he woke up so many times as if someone has touched his shoulder. The numbers didn't make any sense to him, but it only took me a few minutes to understand their meaning. Our children's birthdays! Billy's birthday is 1/07, Philip's is 2/19, Jim's son Phillip's birthday is 3/20 and John's birthday is 5/04. All these numbers came through to Jim before we knew about each other!

Every place we have lived since we've been married has had the number 55 in the address without our looking ahead of time! (Six addresses!) We find many 55's these days and still don't understand how they all fit, but as I write this book I'm 55 years old. I've written 55 chapters without planning it! (When I started writing the book, I was afraid it wouldn't be long enough!) I firmly believe that my 55$^{th}$ year holds great promise.

No one knows what the future holds for any of us, but I encourage each of you to take control of your life now. Start making those dreams come true. Make a list of your goals. Take steps every day to create something you always wanted. Somewhere along the way, perhaps because of difficult lessons learned, this book will encourage others who are making difficult choices or feel like they have no hope or a way out of a bad situation.

It's easy to feel like you are the only person in the world who is going through bad times. You may feel that you are alone in your sorrow or grief.

You say, "I don't deserve anything better. There's no way out! Everybody else can, but I can't. No one knows the truth. I'm stuck with what I have. It's too late now. I'm too old. I can't do it alone. I'm not good enough. I've done too many bad things. Who cares, anyway?"

I've thought every single one of those statements in my lifetime! None of those excuses are true! It's all just a mindset that we can change in a moment!

All my life I've been surrounded by people who thought I was sweet and loving and kind, but most didn't think about how much I needed to hear the words of encouragement or thanks for a job well done. Few realized I was tormented with fear of failure and even fewer took the time to give praise when it was due.

When I was running for the elected position of township clerk, one of my first goals was to feel positive about myself. I wrote messages on the bathroom mirror. "You are special." "You are successful!" "You can do it!" When the shower's mist covered the words, I traced them with my fingers. Even after years of therapy with Dr. Berecz, I struggled to believe in myself. I think Dr. B knew that I would never be able to rise above that obsession as long as I lived with someone who didn't believe in me, but he knew it wasn't for him to make that choice.

When I resigned from being the local newspaper correspondent, I was absolutely shocked to discover how many people thought I'd done an outstanding job.

On March 1, 1991 when the Chief of Police, Jim Kesterke, found out I wouldn't be responding to accidents and fires he was surprised that the newspaper let me quit. "I thought you'd get a promotion. You write with such a passion," he said.

The Berrien Springs Schools Superintendent, Tedd Morris, told me that few people could stand up for something with such honesty as I had done.

Bob Pagel, the township superintendent had tears in his eyes when he found out that I wouldn't be covering the township board meetings anymore. "Something bigger and better will happen," he assured me.

The police dispatcher asked me if I had contacted a TV station. "You have so much talent!" she said.

Shockingly, the day before I had written in my diary, *"Cry and you cry alone."*

I had no idea that I was so much appreciated.

Do not condemn yourself for needing gentle encouragement and praise along the way. That's a good sign that you are a sensitive and caring individual. Place yourself in situations where you get the good words and pats on the back as often as you need them.

If your boss is insensitive and ungrateful, get another job. If your significant other is selfish, inconsiderate and demanding, you should decide if the relationship is worth it. If your children make demands on your time and energy, find the courage to just say no. If friends and relatives always take and don't give back in return, let them go! If your church isn't offering peace, find another church.

Have you found your golden nuggets? I know that every human being on earth has golden nuggets that beg to be appreciated. Anyone who has read to this section of this book has found something that has touched your heart. If I have held your interest, it is because you have related to my journey. Have you walked in my shoes and

.nd comfortable?  Or, have you stumbled and
.les as you tried to walk in shoes that did not fit?
es I am asked why I don't hold grudges or feel
.gry at those who have wronged me. Why I don't
ght back when I'm judged harshly.

they wronged me? As one of my sweet patients said when she was reading this book before publication, "It's how you react to the bad things that happen in your life that make the difference."

Only the mystery of the universe can remember the millions of people I have touched or been touched by, on my life's journey. However brief or long; happy or sad; frustrating or content; sickness or in health; wanted or not wanted. Each moment in time or person along the way had a purpose in my life.

Did grandma harbor any golden nuggets?  There are those who will say she made a positive impact on their lives and they respect her memory with honor.  Sandra and I know a few by name who would confirm that.

I close this book by asking you to search for your golden nuggets of purpose, courage, hope and peace.  I wish I could find them for you, but you must find your own!

To those reading this book who need encouragement to find your way, please feel free to email me on the Internet.

My email address is http://www.lindasbook@usa.com

My website (blog) address is http://dustyangels.blogspot. com

My photography website is photosbylinda.com

Before I leave you now, I'd like to share with you a special loving verse that Jim sent to me on September 29, 1997, as we were getting to know each other via the Internet before we had met for the first time.

This loving message applies to anyone walking the journey of life today.

## Celestial Wanderers

"Step out your back door and look to the horizon's edge in
the southwest.
Shining bright in the sky will be Venus and slightly up and to
the left is Mars.
They have been 'reaching out' to each other all summer and
are only now coming close enough to be touched by a beam of
loving light.
Perhaps, we too are like those celestial wanderers, only a wee
bit closer to home.
For in our solitudes of mutual wanderings, we too have
reached out over the vast presence of cyberspace and, having
come into conjunction, now have the cosmic opportunity to
'touch' each other's life and create a mutual destiny.
A wee bit like being touched by an ANGEL called:  Linda

"The End"

Linda & James Meikle
5514 Sweetwater Valley Circle
New Albany, OH 43054

* CRAig
Sandra Zike
6513 S. Englewood Ave.
Tampa, FL 33611
813 831-7884

# Quick Order Form

AuthorHouse online store: www.authorhouse.com

The author's website: www.lindasbookshelf.com

Dusty Angels and Old Diaries by Linda J. Meikle is available through 25,000 retail outlets worldwide, on the Internet via Amazon. com, Barnes&Noble.com and Borders.com.

Through Ebay at Angelwings Attic Store (Exact cost at this site.)

Call toll-free for information 1-888-854-7522. Ask for Linda Meikle.

The cost through the author is $12.95 plus $2.00 S/H Media Mail. Add $1.00 shipping for each additional book ordered. Indicate who you would like the book(s) autographed to.

Linda's cell ph.
614 329-7513

HHP://dustyangels.blogspot.com

Love, Linda

# About the Author. . .

Linda has worked as A Licensed Practical Nurse since 1971 and is an entrepreneur and writer at heart. Dusty Angels and Old Diaries is her first published book created from a lifetime of diaries and journals. A professional photographer for many years, her first photography business opened in 1989 as Magic Moments Photography. She was a local newspaper correspondent for the Herald-Palladium in St. Joseph, Michigan, and won two elections as the Oronoko Township Clerk in Berrien Springs, Michigan. After almost 40 years of searching, Linda found her mother and seven siblings! She is a published poet, award-winning photographer, ham radio operator and musician. She has two sons and two stepsons. Linda and her husband James live in the Midwest with two faithful dogs and one sleepy black cat.

Printed in the United States
103355LV00003B/172-180/A

9 781425 907235